Closed Sea

Closed Sea
From the Manasquan to the Mullica
A History of Barnegat Bay

Kent Mountford

DOWN
THE
SHORE
PUBLISHING

West Creek, New Jersey

Down The Shore Publishing, Box 100, West Creek, NJ 08092
www.down-the-shore.com

*The words "Down The Shore" and the Down The Shore Publishing logos
are registered U.S. Trademarks.*

Manufactured in the United States of America.
10 9 8 7 6 5 4

Book design by Leslee Ganss.
Cover photograph by the author.

Library of Congress Cataloging-in-Publication Data
Mountford, Kent, 1938-

Closed Sea; from the Manasquan to the Mullica: a history of Barnegat Bay / Kent Mountford
    p. cm.
Includes bibliographical references and index.
ISBN 0-945582-84-6 (hc)

1. Barnegat Bay Region (N.J.) --History. 2. Barnegat Bay Region (N..J.)--Discovery and exploration. I. title.

F142.O2 M68 2002
974.9'48--dc21

                                                    2002020816

ISBN 1-59322-027-8 (trade paper)
ISBN-13 978-1-59322-027-3

*Publication of this book is made possible, in part, by a Barnegat Bay Estuary Program mini-grant,
administered by the Tuckerton Seaport with support from the Ocean County Historical Society.*

To Dorothy Elinor Gordon Mountford-Sage

A life spanning most of the last century, begun in the year the Titanic sank and onward onto the new millennium. Loyal, sometimes challenging wife to two husbands, over six decades. Tenacious mother to one son (me), a dog, and two cats; tolerant sometime-keeper of a canary, hamsters, numerous mice, snakes, fish, hand-tamed chipmunks, songbirds and neighborhood raccoons.

Contents

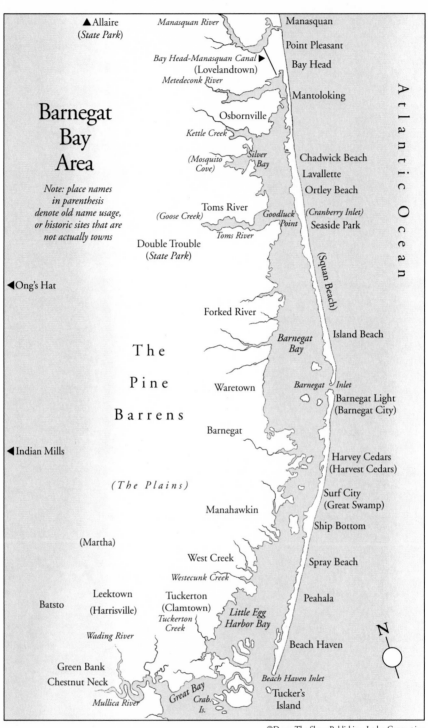

▲Allaire
(State Park)

Manasquan River

Manasquan

Point Pleasant

Bay Head-Manasquan Canal ▶
(Lovelandtown)
Metedeconk River

Bay Head

Mantoloking

Barnegat
Bay
Area

Osbornville

Kettle Creek

*(Mosquito
Cove)*

*Silver
Bay*

Chadwick Beach

Lavallette

Ortley Beach

*Note: place names
in parenthesis
denote old name usage,
or historic sites that are
not actually towns*

Toms River

(Goose Creek)

*Goodluck
Point*

(Cranberry Inlet)

Seaside Park

Toms River

Double Trouble
(State Park)

◀Ong's Hat

Forked River

Barnegat
Bay

Island Beach

T h e

P i n e

Waretown

Barnegat ⌣Inlet

Barnegat Light
(Barnegat City)

B a r r e n s

Barnegat

◀Indian Mills

Harvey Cedars
(Harvest Cedars)

(The Plains)

Surf City
(Great Swamp)

Manahawkin

Ship Bottom

(Martha)

West Creek

Spray Beach

Westecunk Creek

Leektown
(Harrisville)

Tuckerton
(Clamtown)

Peahala

Batsto

*Tuckerton
Creek*

*Little Egg
Harbor Bay*

Wading River

Green Bank

Chestnut Neck

Beach Haven

Beach Haven Inlet

Mullica River

Great Bay

*Crab.
Is.*

⟲Tucker's
Island

N

Atlantic Ocean

(Squan Beach)

Introduction

This book survived as an unpublished manuscript for over four decades. Written in the late 1950s, the work now reaches a broad readership, at a time of great new interest in the history and ecology of the Barnegat Bay region.

1960

Protected from a turbulent Atlantic by the pale sandy arms of a barrier beach, Barnegat Bay lies along the seacoast of New Jersey and is taken much for granted by an urban society exploiting it only towards hedonistic ends.

As a small boy in 1946, I admit a similar motivation when from the bow of the old charter boat *Duchess II* I first beheld an evening Barnegat through the unopened portals of Mantoloking Bridge. To my chagrin, a power failure prevented this barrier from yielding to the captain's repeated horn blasts. The *Duchess* had high and easily lowered fishing outriggers — the only reason we needed the bridge to open — and, power failure or not, the bridge tender's angry words fell memorably on my young ears: "I wouldn't open for no goddamned bamboo stick anyhow!" We headed back to Brielle through the Bay Head-Manasquan Canal.

In the 1950s, sailing aboard my uncle's stable little catboat *Osprey*, I came to regard Barnegat's turbid waters as a springboard from which I would one day sally forth upon the great Atlantic. But with time, and my own sailboats, I became conditioned to a Barnegat life and recognized this Bay was more than enough challenge for my frail barks.

One day I pulled up an old bait-box and opening it exposed for me the Bay's teeming world of marine wonders. Later, when a required freshman English course at Rutgers University found me in quest of a research paper topic, I chose to write about Barnegat's marine life, a subject which since the baitbox had fascinated me. I titled that paper "Closed Sea". The professor, intolerant of its indifferent spelling and dangling clauses, rated my work poorly. It had nonetheless been such a labor of love that independent of my college curriculum, I began writing what has become this book.

The name "Closed Sea" came from a legal term, the Latin *Mare clausum*, which I encountered during my business law course, but it is exactly on the mark describing an estuary, a partially enclosed body of water having riverine inputs and tidal exchange with the adjacent ocean.

The beach and pines have known my tread three score seasons now, and the bay's waters my keel for a decade. This is the story of the closed sea those waters comprise: a varied tale of Vikings and inlets, cranberries and cannon, a tale of time, life and mankind.

What I have chosen to call the "Barnegat area" is at best an arbitrary thing, but loath as I am to chop off the bay at Manahawkin, I have allowed her influence to extend generously behind the sea islands, with a convenient bit of overlap at each end, describing something more than the boundaries of Ocean County.

Try as I might to halt it, the story never really stopped growing; there was always something new to add. The tale is never fully told. Why tell it? George Leigh Mallory said of the mighty Everest: "...because it is there."

This *has* been a labor of love, and its satisfaction lay in the growth of my own understanding, the perceptions of inter-relationships between past and present, between life and environment. Here must lie the joy of such work, far outweighing the pride of publication, or of communicating to others what I wished to say.

Kent Mountford, 1960

2002

Jersey's beaches and pines have known my tread for more than three score years now, and the waters my keel past five decades. So many more miles sailed, more than 30,000: from Maine, through New England, the Virgin Islands, Bahamas, Martinique, on the Sulu and South China seas, the great Chesapeake Bay ... and many summers drawn back again and again to old Barnegat.

I read this book now from a perspective of four decades distance, and a lot has changed in that time. Not much for the better, the intervening years telling their own sad story of careless destruction; the taking away of history and loss of once vibrant habitat. Population has grown almost exponentially since the 1950s, and the Bay suffers from it. Speech accents once uniquely "Piney" in timbre are today often indistinguishable from New York or North Jersey.

Old Barnegat, the one I remember back a half century, is gone. We are also a long way from 1960, when I wrote the first introduction to this completed manuscript, but it is a re-awakening of public interest in community history and in restoration of the Barnegat Bay ecosystem which now permits the book to see light today.

Closed Sea, in its growth, consumed several years, a profound undertaking for a young man in the first quarter century of his life. It spoke a worshipful attachment to the sea, and its relation to the land, one which has never left me. I wrote then, in 1960, about that bond and how close it held me:

"When we hold to our ear a shell, no matter how alienated from the mother sea, we hear still the thunder of roaring surf. But, it is not the sea we hear but the blood in our veins that rises and falls only on the tide of emotion. How far removed are we from that primordial sea, the genesis of all life? Even in that very blood we bear chemical vestiges of a former oceanic being. Perhaps from the involute recesses of the empty shell, we do hear the sea, locked in us and moving us, who knows how far or fast, in sympathy with that ancient mother..."

Closed Sea was to have a second volume, one which would describe the bay's marine and seashore life, but I realize in the 1960s that, though such a volume would be useful, I did not yet know enough to instruct others. Within a few years I was immersed in serious study of this Bay's ecology, work that consumed the following decade and ended with M.S. and Ph.D. degrees from Rutgers. A research job with the Academy of Natural Sciences in Philadelphia then took me to a rural field station on the vast Chesapeake estuary, which has held me as sailor and scientist for more than three decades — a decade in the private sector and academia and two decades in government, working for that bay's future.

I hope you enjoy *Closed Sea*. It speaks, some years before its time, to the relatively recent discipline of environmental history, a subject that is now the major focus of my professional life.

Kent Mountford
February, 2002

Chapter 1

They Led
The Way

The Norseman

It was, perhaps, a morning in August, the year, AD 1011. The shoals off Barnegat were calm at slack tide, brushed only by the catspaws of an indefinite morning breeze. Eastward, resting on the sea, was the long dragon-ship of Thorfinn Karlsefni. Her ornate sail panting slowly in the calm heat, she lay waiting for a south wind to bear her up the coast.

Hauk Book, from the many volumes of Norse sagas, tells us that Karlsefni, having spent the previous winter in the sheltered Hudson River — which on discovering he called *Straumfiord* — set out with the coming of April and worked southward with two or three of his ships. Here his party entered Chesapeake Bay, naming part of it *H'op* and remaining a time in that land. Towards August, Thorfinn coasted northward, born close inshore by the prevailing southerlies.

It was against the true Viking code to ignore any sizeable break in a coastline, so it is probable that Karlsefni entered our coast at least in the Delaware. It would also be convenient to hypothesize his landing at either Egg Harbor or Barnegat, but since this would

[1] The Smithsonian's William Fitzhugh states there is no credible evidence Vikings reached this far south. Others disagree, and still hunt for evidence.

be merely hypothesis,[1] let it suffice that he was probably the first white European to see New Jersey.

The Romans

Marsus Ulpius Traianus was born of a Roman father at Italica, Spain, on September 18, 53 A.D. He ascended as the Roman Emperor Trajan on the death of Nerva, his adoptive father, in 98 A.D. Trajan himself died on campaign at Selinus in Cilicia, August 8, 117 A.D.

Those years were ones of gathering clouds for Rome, and dark, too for the men of some forgotten galley with her purse of coin, driven from the pillars of Hercules across an unknown western ocean to a mythical continent *Lex Romana* would never rule. There, on unseen shoals south of Barnegat, their ship fell into disfavor with the gods and was crushed by a merciless surf.

For some eighteen hundred years her memory lay secreted beneath the Atlantic until one morning, after the gods had rekindled their timeless wrath on the face of the sea, a coin was left on the sands, and then more coins. Was there a ship? There were still coins in the 1950s, and, following the dark, pounding storms, they found their way to light.[2]

[2] You can see a bronze Roman coin at the Barnegat Light Museum, in addition to Spanish pieces of eight.

The Hoax

An ancient letter, written in Normandy July 8, 1524, to Francis I, from the Florentine adventurer Giovanni da Verrazano, describes a recent and wonderful voyage to a hitherto unrecorded region of the New World. In the document, Verrazano gives a running commentary of his experiences along the coastline from a landfall at Cape Roman north to Nova Scotia. He notes what proved to be New Jersey, calling it "New France," and would lead one to believe that he was first, or, by our calculations, next, to meander along our shore. The letter was apparently the only record of the voyage that could be considered an original account, but the claim it espouses has retained almost unquestioned credulity in the eyes of modern historians.

We are told, however, that while supposedly making his discovery, the omnipresent Giovanni was engaged in certain corsairial endeavors for the King of Spain in another part of the world. Of course, this report could have been erroneous, but further doubt may be cast on the discovery by critical examination of the Verrazano letter itself.

First we must consider the factor of time. The purported expedition left Nova Scotia for Europe sometime in June, but that was long after the crew members averred partaking of local grapes. We find that the earliest grapes on our shores bear fruit no earlier than July. The document also contains certain inaccurate representations as to the inhabitants of the coast and their customs which, in the interests of brevity, I shall omit.

In the general area of Long Island, Verrazano claimed to have found "the Isles of Louise," named conveniently after King Francis' doting mother and represented as being some 400-square miles in extent.

According to historian Henry Murphy,[3] Verrazano, in all probability, did not even claim the discovery, but rather was used as a pawn by desperate Florentine merchants who sought to bolster the crumbling prestige of their decaying city-state. But where did the author, be he Giovanni or some 15th century ghost writer, get his information? Much is too accurate to have been fabricated, for we see not only the Highlands and the Hudson, but even a Jersey which he calls "New France." The problem is apparently resolved by reference to the writings of one Est'evan Gomez.

[3]*You must read Murphy to evaluate for yourself. Others support Verrazano, and so the New York bridge bears his name.*

Est'evan Gomez, Portuguese Viking

Gomez was a Portuguese pilot — in fact chief pilot — for the intrepid Magellan, at the start of the latter's globe-encircling voyage. For reasons undefined, however, Gomez broke away from the fleet and, perhaps foolishly, returned to Spain, where he was promptly thrown in jail. There he remained in some ignominy until the arrival of the *Vittoria*, survivor of the five original ships, at Seville in September of 1522. Magellan was dead and a paltry eighteen Europeans were left. It was probably fortunate for Est'evan that Magellan was dead, for following the customary bureaucratic delays, he was released on issuance of a *cedula*, August 27, 1523.

Gomez enters our story sometime in February of 1525 when, in a tiny blundering caravel of fifty "tonnes" burden, he set sail across the western ocean. It appears that it was this exploration from which the Verrazzano letter arose.

Sailing northward from a landfall on the coast of North America, Est'evan entered the Delaware, marking also the Highlands and the mighty Hudson. Upon his return to Europe, the results of his voyage were made public both in France and Spain. A chart drawn from the data by one Hizola Diego Ribero, published in 1529 and thus postdating both individual's claims, denotes our seaboard in sweeping characters: *Tiera de Esteva Gomez*. It would appear that at least one contemporary of both men recognized the claim of Gomez; perhaps it would be well for history to take another look at the purported statements of our (possibly) less-venturesome Florentine.

A Passing Reference

In the Verrazano letter (which we may assume to be the gleanings from Est'evan Gomez) is a reference which leads historians to believe that Verrazano, or if you will, Gomez, had entered and explored the Mullica River. The natives are mentioned, as are local pigeons that darkened the sky with their flight. The writings dwell, momentarily, on a land of "many lakes and ponds of living water." One hangs eagerly on such a phrase, searching for an embryonic description of Barnegat Bay. Perhaps this was it, but for all intents and purposes, the "Closed Sea" remained a closed book for some 598 years after Thorfinn Karlsefni braved our shoreline, until the pen of one Robert Juet exposed it to the world.

Chapter 2

Of Burning Hole

Derde Reize (The Third Journey)

The inlet of Barnegat first makes her debut in the journal of an Englishman, Robert Juet, who acted as mate (or to some, keeper of the log) for Hendrik Hudson during his memorable third voyage to the New World. Their ship was the rotund but worthy *Halve Maan*, displacing about 96 metric tons and making a meager four knots on the wind, perhaps seven knots off their mission; "...seeking a Northwest passage to China" for the great and venerable Dutch East India Company.

As they enter our tale, the voyagers have left Cape Henlopen and borne northward to a position somewhat above latitude 39° 3' N. The date is September 2, 1609:

> The Second, in the morning close weather, the winde at South in the morning; from twelve untill two of the clocke we steered North North-west, and had sounding one and twentie fathoms, and in running one Glasse[1] we had but sixteene fathoms, then seventeene, and so Shoalder and Shoalder untill it came to twelve

[1] *The time between turnings of the ships hourglass.*

fathoms. We saw a great Fire, but could not see the Land, then we came to ten fathoms, whereupon we took our tackes aboord, and stood to the Eastward East South-east, foure Glasses. Then the Sunne arose, and we Steered away North againe, and saw Land from the West by North, to the Northwest by North, all like broken islands, and our soundings were eleven and ten fathoms. Then wee loosed in for the shoare, and fair by the shoare, we had seven fathoms. The course along the Land we found to be North-east by North. From the land we first had sight of, untill we came to a great Lake of water, as wee could judge it to bee, being drowned Land, which made it to rise like Ilands, which was in length ten leagues. The mouth of that Lake hath many shoalds, and the sea breaketh on them as it is cast out of the mouth of it. And from that Lake or Bay, the Land lyeth North by East, and wee had a great streame out of the Bay; and from thence our sounding was ten fathoms, two leagues from the Land. At five of the clocke we anchored, being little winds, and rode in eight fathoms of water, the night was faire. This night I found the Land to hall the Compasse 8°. For to the Northward off us we saw high Hils. For the day before we found not above 2° of Variation. This is a very good Land to fall in with, and a pleasant Land to see.

Thus friend Robert set aside his pen, extinguished a gently swinging lantern, and, no doubt, swatting a few Jersey mosquitoes, rolled into his bunk, leaving Barnegat Bay now recorded for posterity.

Apparently others on board marked the region in some detail, for further insights emerge in J. DeVaet's *Nieuwe Werelt*, brought forth in 1625:

> ...from this cape they saw land ENE, which they thought to be an island, but (then) found the vast land and the twin capes of the bay (Delaware Bay, Cape May), at (a) height of 38° 54' (N. Latitude) and from there they held a course NW then N, here they found the land to be embayed and noted many breakers, so they again stood out SSE. They conjectured that there a great river must flow, judging by the great stream (that) set out of there...stretching from this place along the shore was a white sandy beach (Island Beach), and being all drowned land and being land all full trees...

Somewhat more enthusiastic than Juet's account, we find the mention of "such a high land as they had never seen and a high cape... after which a bay lay." This was probably Atlantic Highlands and, of course, Sandy Hook Bay.

Our gateway to the Atlantic came thus to the eyes of the world, variously hypothesized to be a lake, bay, or river. In all accounts, we find her characterized as a turbulent mass of shoals and breakers, over which rolled the tides of Barnegat. Though marked, the inlet still bore no title, nor would she for many years.

Captains Mey and Hendrickson

Following early explorations of the New World, the Dutch, who are, after all, a shrewd folk, established the West India Company and set their sights on one Cornelius Jacobsen Mey, of Hoorn, Netherlands, commissioning him for a "southerly voyage of exploration" in the ship *Fortuyn*. He thus sailed from New Amsterdam in June of 1614.

With the advancing months of that year, Mey poked his nose southward along the middle Atlantic coast, marking Absecon Inlet (from the Lenape *Absegami*, or "Little Water") and Barnegat, too, with the cryptic warning *barende-gat* — "breaking inlet."

But, with the lack of precision that ordinarily accompanies transcription, we find a chart of Adrian Vanderdonck's which, in 1656, shows *barende-gat* construed for the first time, into a name "Barndegat." Absecon has become "Bear-Gat." Shortly thereafter a chart generally ascribed to the same gentleman resolves the inconsistency, labeling both inlets "Barndegat." The consistency is short lived, however, for by 1671 Arnoldus Montanus, in his map of New Belgium, wanders still further from the original with "Burndegat."

While cartographers in Europe were struggling, however feebly, with the challenges of nomenclature, knowledge of more pertinent physical characteristics had been gathered by an enterprising fellow named Cornelius Hendrickson. It seems that while Captain Mey was wending his way homeward in 1614, a bluff bowed and sloop-rigged shallop was constructed in the budding settlement of New Amsterdam. The *Onrest* ("restless") as she was known, rode lightly and drew little water, characteristics of the *Nederlandsche Hoogars* after which she was patterned. Her builder and skipper, Captain Adrian Block, sailed her through Long Island Sound, where he found, and appropriately named Block Island. Returning to New Amsterdam, Block then sold *Onrest* to

Hendrickson, who provisioned her for an exploratory voyage along the coast of New Jersey. Butting out into the Atlantic one morning, the little sloop became the first ocean-going vessel to be constructed on the eastern seaboard of North America.

Probably no more than a day later, Hendrickson sounded Barnegat Inlet and entered the bay, closely noting the tributaries that fed into it. Then proceeding south, he left a lookout stationed on Cape May and returned subsequently to harbor in the Hudson River. Shortly thereafter, his map was made public in Holland, where the data proved more accurate than any available for the next half century.

Of Burning Hole

I now introduce the product of John Seller and William Fisher, *A Mapp of New Iarsey* {Jersey} *in America,* (London, 1676 or 1677). Their contribution to the mutation of *barende-gat* is "Burning Hole."

This presents, it would appear, a problem somewhat deeper than spelling, for a new idea seems to have emerged. Perhaps there was a connection between the two; that is, in the linguistically ignorant mind, the transformation might follow: "barende-gat" to "Burning Gap," and finally, "Burning Hole." However, I felt somehow unsatisfied with this explanation and for some time sought in vain for a better answer. Then a sentence in Juet's writings caught my eye and led me to the hypothesis that "Burning Hole" might bear no relation to the original form.

A *New* Halve Maan

In 1909, to commemorate the three-hundreth anniversary of Hudson's voyage, a reproduction of the *Halve Maan*, or *Half Moon*, was constructed, as accurately as history would allow.[2] The following illustration shows her as she was that year.

She had a tarred bottom, undecorated brown topsides and gilded trailboards. Her transom was blue with waning moon and scattered stars, as shown. The ship, probably sailing as well as the original, made four knots on the wind and around seven running be-

[2] *Yet another Half Moon was built late in the 20th century, and still sails the coast as a goodwill ambassador.*

A sketch of the Halve Maan, *showing how she appeared in 1909.*

Draft: 1.749 meters (5.75 ºft.) for'd. 2.135 meters (7.2 ft.) aft
Length: between Perpendiculars 17.832 meters (58.6 ft.)
Greatest Beam: 4.940 metric tons (16.24 ft.)
Displacement: 95.9 metric tons (1000 kg.) 30 tons ballast

fore it. As was the custom in those days, she carried six guns, including two swivels and a pair of "chasers," which were aimed through the transom in order to discourage or hamper pursuit. A 12-foot sloop, corresponding to the latter day longboat, was carried athwartships on chocks.

When, in 1609, Hendrik Hudson returned from his *Derde Reiz* to the New World, a Spanish cartographer, Don Alonso De Velasco, codified the data collected and composed a chart, showing where the coastline was visited by the *Halve Maan*. In the chart, New Jersey has clearly the mark of Barnegat Bay, cutting into the shore quite like the river spoken of. This is the earliest known "chart" of the bay, hardly adequate by modern standards, but nevertheless of historical worth. The breaking shoals, despite their prominence in later years, are apparently represented by the two small dashes at the inlet's mouth.

Let us hark back briefly to September 2, 1609. Once again Robert Juet speaks:

> ...and we saw a great Fire, but could not see the Land..., whereupon we brought our tackes aboord and stood to the Eastward East South-east, foure Glasses.

Thus, a glass being about half an hour, and their ship making, let us say, four knots into the southerly, at daybreak the *Halve Maan* lay about eight nautical miles ESE of the "great Fire." Bearing north again, the ship ran inshore, sighting land somewhere between present-day Surf City and Harvey Cedars. This was but a little south of Barnegat Inlet.

To me, it did not seem inconceivable that later mariners, seeking a name for the opening, might have connected the fire and the inlet, especially since neither Juet nor Hudson, nor in fact Mey, sought to apply one to it. If valid, my little theory would imply that "Burning Hole" was actually the first name purposefully applied to the inlet, but since the records give us no substantiation, the situation is open to conjecture.

Whatever its origins, "Burning Hole," as a name, was to survive at least until the turn of the century. By March 29, 1684, in the testimony of John Barclay and Arthur Forbes, we find "Burning Hole" being used in conjunction with "Barnagat." This document is of interest in that, for the first time it implies future colonization:

> Barnagat or Burning-hole is said to be a very good place for fishing, and there is some desiring to take up land there, who inform that it is good land, and abundance of meadow lying to it.

An attempt at reconciling, or at least making precise the new distinction, is made in 1690 by the *Phillip Lea Chart*, with "Burnegat or Burning Hole." About 1700, John Worlidge, in his extensive *New Map of East and West Jersey as Surveyed by* ...(etc.), is the first to recognize Barnegat Bay, as such. He still, however, denotes the inlet as Burning Hole.

From a map in Samuel Smith's *History of the Colony of Nova Caesaria* (1765), which was drawn in 1747, we appear to pinpoint the demise of Burning Hole, for the inlet is now called "Burnigat, commonly called Barnegat." But while custom had now established Barnegat as the accepted form, William Faden of Charing

Cross felt obligated to distort just once more. In his map, *The Province of New Jersey, Divided into East and West — Commonly Called the Jerseys*, he carefully printed a "Barnigate Inlet" opening into "The Sound" which lay behind "Old Barnegat Beach," the latter term being perhaps a concession to popular usage.

In Later Years

But ultimately, "Barnegat" triumphed, a far cry from "barendegat," but possibly a little closer than "Burning Hole." In 1800, the *American Coast Pilot* is quoted, showing rather clearly the extent to which the seaman had now to reckon with our inlet's treacherous shallows:

> The shoal of Barnegat does not extend beyond three miles from the beach and is very steep too; you may turn this shoal in six fathoms of water within pistol shot of the outward breakers.... By passing Barnegat in the daytime it may easily be known, should you be so far off as not to see the breakers; you will see a long wood back in the Country, apparently three or four miles long, known to the coasters by the name of Little Swamp and lies directly to the rear of the Inlet of Barnegat.

Mr. Blunt's text appears almost apologetic, as if trying to deride the terror-ridden tales which were told of the "'Gat;" and well he might. The shoals had taken, and were to continue to take a great toll in ships and human life.

Chapter 3

Harbors: Something Old, Something New

Our Modest Captain Mey

Nineteen miles south of Barnegat Inlet, at the lower extreme of Long Beach Island and opening eastward from the broad expanse of Little Egg Harbor, lies another gateway to the sea — or is it two? It was two a few years ago, but back three centuries it was only one, and that one was neither of the two latter-day inlets.

Captain Mey sailed southward skirting "ye shoalds" of Barnegat, in the summer of 1614. His ship, the *Fortuyn*, was one of five belonging to the West India Company at that time and he was no doubt loathe to risk ripping her bottom out on a sandbar. But below Barnegat Bay, he found a broad blue inlet with sufficient water for his craft and, being the explorer he was, ghosted in under topsails to look around. Anchoring in a commodious harbor, he sent a boat and some of his men ashore.

The beaches, at that season, were overwhelmed with the eggs and young of countless breeding sea birds. So impressed were Mey and his men, they named the place "Eyer Haven" or Egg Harbor. The group, picking their way amongst the jammed rookeries, were probably the first caucasians to walk on Long Beach Island.

Sailing southward once more, Mey and his crew came upon still another fine harbor, and landing, discovered more colonies of sea birds. These may have been of a larger sort having larger eggs, for the voyageurs named it Great Egg Harbor, correspondingly revising the northern port to Little Egg Harbor.

Fourteen years after Hendrik Hudson in 1623, Mey made another pass along the shore in the *Blyde Broodschap* ("glad tidings"), also of the West India Company and, following a propensity which we are told was his, "discovered" and named "Cape Mey" after himself. Putting ashore he found the lookout Hendrickson had established some nine years earlier. But the name he'd given the place stuck, with only slight anglicization, and is today Cape May.

In Later Years

Ten years later another Dutch navigator, David Pieterzen de Vries, sailed through the great inlet and up the silent river that wound inland, south of Little Egg Harbor. From the Indians he met, he found the name of this river to be *Amintonck* (which, as a town name, survives to this day at the headwaters of the river, anglicized as "Hammonton"). The voyagers were astounded by a great flock of pigeons that literally darkened the sky with their flight. These were the carrier pigeons European Americans subsequently hunted to extinction.

Eric Mullica

Since the Amintonck is now called the Mullica, we must make reference to a couple of Swedish ships that crept up the Delaware in 1638. They were the man o' war *Kalmar Nyckel*[1] and the sloop *Gripen* which brought some of their countrymen to settle in the New World. Amongst those aboard was a 15-year old lad named Eric Mullica. In 1645, as a young man, Mullica would lead a band of settlers to a spot along the north bank of Amintonck, about fifteen miles from the bay.

[1] A 350-ton replica of the Kalmar Nyckel was commissioned and sailing in 1998. Her home port is Wilmington, Delaware.

Although the Swedes in the Delaware colony were, in later years, driven out by a plague of Jersey mosquitoes, Mullica and his hardy followers remained. Eric himself proved quite a memorable character, dying at the age of one hundred in 1723. The Mullica River, it goes without saying, bears his correct name today, notwithstanding valiant efforts by cartographers in the interim: 1678, "Muliicus," survey of 1726, "Mollicas," and later still, 1777, "Mullicus."

Inlets Old and New

The inlet which opened to the sea from Little Egg Harbor and the Mullica became known warmly as "Old Inlet," wide of channel and better than a mile wide between the two beaches that flanked it. To the south was so-called "Short Beach" and to the north, "Long Beach," which extended its lengthy arm to the edge of Barnegat Inlet some eighteen miles away. In 1656 cartographer Adrian Vanderdonck speaks of the region surrounding, and to the north, as "Eyerhaven at Beyehaven:"

> There are several fine bays and inland waters... which at present are not very much used, particularly Barndegat... and Little Egg Harbor... as there are few Christians settled at those places.

But in a few decades and, indeed, all through the period of the American Revolution, the "fine bays and inland waters" prospered and became a critical route for trade and supply. For the vast part of two centuries, Old Inlet was considered the finest passage on the Jersey coast. As late as the period 1803-1812, vessels drawing 15- to 18-feet brought cargos into Egg Harbor, attesting to at least that much water over the bar at high water.

But, in the year 1800, the death-knell of Old Inlet was sounded. Some six or eight miles south, amongst the battered dunes along Short Beach lay a depressed swale covered with a scrub of red cedars. One night the pounding fury of a northeast storm sliced through the depression, forming, with the dawn, a swirling new inlet. Usurping the tidal flow, "New Inlet" widened and deepened leaving the old inlet to dwindle away.

In 1815, Blunt's *American Coast Pilot* shows two fathoms in Old Inlet but, by 1827, a subsequent edition of the same book has an insert of "Tucker's Beach," which locals named the island created by the opening of New Inlet. The chart takes a bearing on the Tucker homestead and a comment directs ships drawing less than 6 1/2-feet north to Old Inlet. And so it continued, so that by 1874, sand from the tip of Long Beach Island had drifted down on the littoral current, so close to Tucker's Beach that one could wade

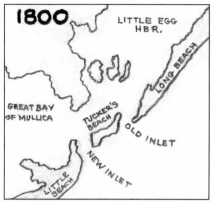

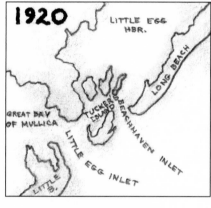

*The changing scene
around
Little Egg Harbor
1750 -1960*

scale approximate

across at low tide. Four years later, only a tiny gap remained, crooked beneath a slowly extending split of sand. Before long, even that had disappeared, fusing Long Beach and Tucker's Beach for the first time in recorded history.

Now unhindered by competition for the tidal flux, "New Inlet" soon assumed the role of its predecessor. During the 19th century (sometime in the latter half, to be as exact as possible), local sages deemed "New Inlet" no longer new and assigned the present day name of "Little Egg Harbor Inlet," after the body of water into which it led.

The story, however, does not end here, for on February 4, 1920, a fierce winter storm again severed the frail bond between Tucker's Beach and Long Beach Island. Tucker's Beach became now "Tucker's Island," and a new "Old Inlet" flowed out to the sea. Taking their cue from a nearby community, locals dubbed the re-born passage "Beach Haven Inlet."

[2] In recent years, "Tucker's Island" has re-emerged from the sea, and by 2000 was again a picnic spot for recreational boaters.

This time the lot fell to Tucker's Island, rather than the opposing Little Egg Inlet, to suffer the ravages of tide and time, and for many years it clung precariously to existence as the inlets licked away at its unprotected flanks. In 1958, it disappeared beneath the surface[2] and for the time being at least, the inlets have become one: something old and something new.

Chapter 4

Cranberry and The Captains

About a Vanishing Inlet

In the later years of his life, David Mapes resided as a respected Black Quaker in Tuckerton, but, as a boy, he was employed by a Mr. Solomon Wardell to keep cattle on a lonely stretch of Squan Beach, just eastward from the mouth of Toms River. One night during a howling northeast gale, David curled up in his shelter as the cattle nosed together behind the dunes. Awakening the next morning, the boy was astounded to see that during the night an inlet had been scoured through the beach. Mapes made his way quickly back to tiny Toms River village and one can imagine the glee with which his news was received for, week by week, a strong blue tide deepened and broadened the new passage. Strange indeed, that with all this nascent inlet was to mean to them, not a single soul thought to record in what year it opened.

Most authorities maintain that the breakthrough occurred around 1750, but John Worlidge, around 1700, shows an unnamed passage close to the right spot. He supposedly surveyed his own map, so it is unlikely that an inlet could just creep in unnoticed, but an equally scrupulous Phillip Lea in 1747 shows no sign of a passage. Chances are that all three are right; the "experts," Worlidge, and Lea.

Configurations in the geology of the beach and islands in the area show that there must at one time have been an inlet opening from the mouth of the Metedeconk River. This would of course explain the whole thing, but, primarily, by intuition, I feel that this inlet probably predated the colonists, and perhaps even Hendrik Hudson.

Farther south of Toms River, near the spot we call Clearwater[1] today, remnant channels run eastward towards the barrier beach, implying the long forgotten existence of still another opening. These purportedly indicate the course of the "Old Inlet," as it was referred to even early in the 20th century, by aged baymen whose ancestors passed down shadowy references across two centuries. The tale is borne out further by equally vague mention of whalers who, in the 17th century, entered Barnegat Bay through a channel north of "barende-gat." However, these gateways were apparently long-gone when David Mapes dangled his discovery before the eyes of Toms Rivers' budding merchants. It was thus, in 1755, on a map of *The Middle British Colonies of America*, that Thomas Jefferies, Geographer to His Royal Highness Prince of Wales, condescends to recognize the existence of one "New Inlet" at that location.

A New Nomenclature

The appearance of what was first called "New Inlet" radically altered the local scene and, understandably, a few equally new names came about. The whole peninsula, before it was severed, had borne the title Squan Beach. After the inlet cut through, the upper half of the promontory retained this designation and that segment of Barnegat Bay west of it became known as "Flat Bay Sound."

The freshly created island south of Squan Beach, though, was not so easily, nor unanimously titled. Since all the surrounding territory was the colonial possession of Lord Stirling, some of the more opportunistic residents chose to call the strip "Lord Stirling's Beach." The more objective preferred "Nine Mile Beach," and it was many years before a third title, "Island Beach" came into general usage. This name once spread as far north as Bay Head, encompassing practically twice the area originally intended, but today maps show it only referring to the portion between the town of Seaside Park and Barnegat Inlet.

Cranberries

With an inlet opening to the world right under her proverbial nose, it is hardly surprising that little Toms River began to prosper. Her citizens, aware of their advantageous position, turned increasingly to the sea and, before many years had passed, the Water Street wharf was host to heavily laden square-riggers.

Meanwhile, amongst the dunes near "New Inlet," conditions in the low and moist swales were ideal for the growth of cranberries, which shot out their trailing little vines and eagerly bore their crimson fruit. Easily preserved and inherently high in then unknown vitamin C, they were gathered in quantity by an increasing host of Toms River seamen, to be taken as an antiscorbutic[2] on long sea voyages. Coupled, I surmise, with the growing inaptitude of the name "New Inlet," the apparent profusion and obvious utility of the berries prompted a shift to "Cranberry Inlet" sometime after 1777.

Actually, we know very little of the nature of Cranberry Inlet during those years, and what is known comes down in the form of only vague and passing references. Charles Edgar Nash tells us that it was supposedly as wide as Great Egg Harbor Inlet; but he also says the channels were winding, and bars lay off the mouth. Howard D. Van Sant, on the other hand, says it was second only to Egg Harbor Inlet as the finest passage on the Jersey Shore, and by this I assume he would mean the former "Old Inlet." He tells us too, that Cranberry was shallow on the north side but a channel to the south was deep enough to admit large coasters, and ran out in a slightly northeasterly direction. We must naturally ask how large, and this is answered by another source which tells us that ships with four or five masts used to come up to Toms River wharf. They must have drawn at least 10-foot, which rather precludes a more shallow channel for the inlet.

[2]Antiscorbutics — as little as 250 mg. daily — combat the effects of scurvy, a chronic vitamin C deficiency which developes after months of poor diet at sea. Gums bled, wounds failed to heal and weakened men were more vulnerable to cold and heat.

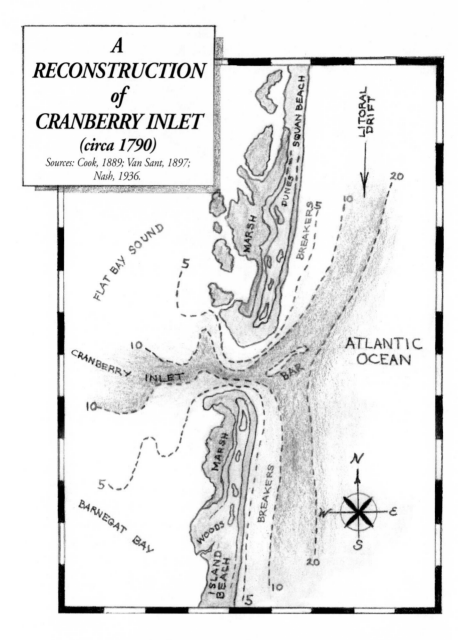

A
RECONSTRUCTION
of
CRANBERRY INLET
(circa 1790)
Sources: Cook, 1889; Van Sant, 1897;
Nash, 1936.

With whatever meager light the above drawing may shed, and a careful study of a topographical survey made about 77 years after the inlet closed, I have attempted, what is to my knowledge, the only reconstruction of Cranberry Inlet in existence. Needless to say, the configurations are more hypothesis than conclusion. Yet, considering how an inlet shapes up under the influence of the currents along our shores, it would not surprise me if some 200-year old local should recognize the accompanying illustration as "ol' Cranberry."

The Captains

With Cranberry Inlet to conduct her ships seaward, Toms River took her place among the increasingly significant seaports on the New Jersey coast. But the very initiative which made her, and, for that matter the rest of the Colonies, grow, led Toms River to participate in events which ultimately brought about the American Revolution.

As a whole, I think, we can consider the period of the American Revolution a profitable one for the little hamlet of Toms River. As a seaport relatively isolated from the areas of major conflict, she, of course, became a supply route for the Continental Army. Perhaps more significant, she lay close to what would then correspond with shipping lanes, fat with rotund British merchant and supply ships en route to New York. Accordingly, Toms River was soon possessed of a privateer horde, and Island Beach became known as one of the most dreaded spots on the Atlantic seaboard.

After the Revolution, an act of the newly established United States government prohibited the use of foreign-built vessels in domestic coastal trade. Accordingly, all along the shore local shipwrights came into their own. Toms River was no exception. Fitted with tough bog iron, framed from the gnarled beach oak, and planked with worm-resistant coastal cedar, many a craft soon parted her first wave in Barnegat Bay's backwaters.

But again in the early years of the 19th century, relations with the Crown strained the bonds of rationality; in 1812, hostilities were renewed. In general, the threat of new depredation by English warships made the cause of battle unpopular with residents of the shore. Nevertheless, the bog forges turned again from kettles to cannon and the economy was swiftly geared for battle.

But in spite of considerable hand rubbing by latent privateers, Toms River did not participate in the War of 1812. For several years, Cranberry's crooked channel had been silting up. The southerly littoral drift had borne increasing amounts of sand southward, shoaling up the waters drastically beyond the mouth. However, it was still an immeasurable shock when one night in 1812, a north-easter closed off the inlet with a broad sandbar. That was that, and the privateers went south to operate out of Little Egg Harbor.

As is perhaps characteristic of humankind, many citizens of Toms River were dissatisfied with nature's high handed decision as to the fate of their home. Michael Ortley, who settled on Island Beach in 1818, belonged to this school. On and off, for some three years, he rallied somewhat reluctant locals to excavate a new Cranberry Inlet a few miles north of the original site. In 1821, Ortly and his companions settled back in satisfaction as a high tide swept in from the Atlantic through their new channel. However, with the next dawn, chagrin replaced satisfaction for the balance of the tide had roundly sealed their hard-earned inlet.

Not so easily daunted, a local Toms River firm turned a sympathetic ear to some of the more traditional thinkers who maintained that a new inlet at the site of old Cranberry might be more successful. So it was that one summer morning, some two or three hundred men under the direction of one Anthony Ivins Jr., tramped out to the spot and began to dig. In a paltry three days, the inlet had been completed. Allowing for a rather conservative channel, a force of men this size, at ten pounds per shovel-full, might have moved 35,000 tons of sand, which I think is quite an achievement for those times.

On the Fourth of July, 1847, with great expostulation about square riggers again forging through Cranberry Inlet, the barrier was opened and a high tide rushed out from Barnegat Bay to mingle with the waters of the Atlantic. One can imagine the continued rejoicing when, a few weeks later, the inlet closed.

Defeated though they were, in two attempts to re-open their gateway to the sea, Toms River captains still could not just turn back to the land and forsake their ships. And so, they sailed south 12-miles to the tortuous channel which led to Barnegat Inlet. Unfortunately even this escape was limited to vessels of shallow draft, and accordingly the shipwright developed a new craft to fill the need: shallow, broad beamed "bay craft." A natural limitation arose, however, in that the bay craft were unsuited for ocean work. Thus, anything destined farther north than Bay Head or south of the Mullica, had to be transferred to coastal schooners. This, coupled with successive declines in the bog iron, cordwood, and charcoal markets, left Toms River with only a fraction of her former significance after the mid-19th century. Whatever the town's adaptations, a hard fact remained; Toms River no longer led to the sea.

One might imagine that the struggle for a new Cranberry might end there, but, in 1835, the state legislature granted a charter for the excavation of a canal to replace Cranberry Inlet by connecting Barnegat Bay and the Manasquan River. This project however, was not completed until 1924, when the Bay Head-Manasquan Canal was opened.

Some Appropriate Irony

On November 17, 1935, as if to flaunt the feeble efforts of years gone by, nature hurled a healthy northeaster up the coast and scoured a sparkling 600-foot channel through the beach between Cranberry and Barnegat. The irony of the situation escaped the attention of prohibition-dried baymen, however, who, having their fill of "near beer" and similar substitutes, turned the passage into a steady stream of imported rum. Guards were posted in a vain attempt to stem the illicit flow. One evening, said patrol, investigating the roar of laboring engines, came upon a craft, anchored by her stern bitts, with props flailing wildly in an attempt to accelerate the tide and deepen the channel. At the intruder's approach, the vessel slipped her moorings and fled across the bay. But guards, rum, or whatever, nature, for the time, at least, had proved the point to her satisfaction and, with spring, the inlet closed.

A sidelight, final to date, came in 1949 or 1950 when still another storm slashed an opening through the barrier somewhere below the Island Beach Coast Guard station. Some unlucky folks were trapped in their shack by the event and, trying to wade the channel, found it was 6-feet deep. Reconnoitering, they decided to wait until a Coast Guard amphibious "duck" trundled across to rescue them. That passage closed rather quickly and the story of Cranberry and the captains ended — until the next time.

Chapter 5

Land of the Lenape

Origin of the Species

There was an ancient legend among certain peoples of the Delaware Nations which purported that mankind had evolved from a race of animals which, in millennia past, enjoyed a subterranean existence. It is told that by some means, a member was one day coughed up from the bowels of the earth and thus the peoples were able to emerge and, with fortune, develop into a functioning civilization. On the basis of this legend, many tribes abstained from eating rabbits, groundhogs, or any of the burrowing animals, lest they partake of some far-removed kin. Early European colonists, not subscribing to this evolutionary hypothesis, believed the Lenape to have evolved from one of the ten original tribes of Judea and, to support their interpretation, they pointed to monotheism, council rule and physical resemblances the two peoples bore.

Present day thought tosses both these ideas aside, having, at least now, a preference for the land-bridge theory, which assumes that at some time during the earth's last glaciation (and a much lower stand of sea level), the Asian and North American land masses were connected across what are today the Bering Straits. Evidence shows man has lived on the North American continent for close to 37,000 years.

The *Walam Olum*, or "red-painted record," corresponds to an official written history of the Lenape. Its tale, traced into pieces of wood and tinted red, follows the tribe as they wander from the forests in the west into the rising sun. Only after many generations did they reached the sea.

Apparently the tribe settled originally in the Hudson Bay area but before many years may have been driven south by the advancing Wisconsin Glaciation. It was thus they came upon this hospitable land (present-day New Jersey) which they called *Scheyechbi* (shay-ak-bee), roughly paraphrased; "long-land-water." Unfortunately, someone was already there.

Big Ones, Too

On the seacoast of *Scheyechbi* lived the *Allegewi*. Near Tuckerton, they dwelt in huts erected on piles in the shallows, and they left behind great mounds of shell, evidence of years of harvesting. The *Allegewi* were a large race, indeed the very name is translated "tall and stout" but their stature was apparently an insufficient bastion against the advancing numbers of the Lenape. Around the turn of the 20th century one of their burial grounds was uncovered, revealing a number of their generous skeletons, entombed with the usual amenities. Some had apparently been killed in battle, maybe with the intrepid Lenape who, at some point in history, overcame, and apparently liquidated, the unfortunate *Allegewi*.

The Lenni Lenape believed themselves (as so many other ethnic groups do) to be the "Original Men" and, appropriately, that is just about what their name means. Their kind were part of the rather extensive and formidable Delaware Nation and, by generalization (if improperly) one will often hear them referred to as "Delawares." Confining ourselves to the coastal areas of New Jersey, we find three distinct subdivisions of the main Lenape stem.

The *Unalachtigo*, or "Turkey," were centered primarily in the southern sector of our state and can be considered as the main agriculturalists. In that region called by the Lenape "middle of the shore," stretching from the Mullica to somewhere above Manahawkin, lived the *Unamis* whose totem was the turtle. Dwelling as they did so near the sea, they were fishermen. The *Unamis*, taking a cue apparently from the defunct *Allegewi*, continued building upon the shell mounds in the marshes south of Tuckerton. The cumulative effect must have been from "tens of centuries," according to authorities, as white men have hauled away the shells for two hundred years with little diminution of the reserve. To the north lay the domains of the *Minisi*, or "Wolf" who, though also generally coastal Indians, were a warlike people. Hendrik Hudson, who lost one of his men to *Minisi* warriors, might not have appreciated the fact, but the tribe was useful to the balance of the Lenape in that they served as a buffer against the equally bellicose Indians of New York and New England. It may seem a bit strange, seeing that the three groups lived within such a relatively small area, but each spoke a distinctly different dialect of the Algonkian tongue.

Children of Manitou

The Lenni Lenape admitted the existence of a single supreme deity, *Manitou*. The *Walam Olum* begins by describing *Manitou* and tells of his creating the sea, sky and earth. The genesis of man and beast hardly needs mention, so close is the parallel with the Judeo-Christian tradition. But for a time evil prevailed and, assuming the configurations of a great serpent, sent a flood across the land. The virtuous forebears of the Lenape, however, rose to safety on the back of a turtle, this possibly being the origin of the *Unamis* totem. If we are to accept such shadowy implications, a great flood may have brought about the early impetus for ancient tribal migrations. Following their providential delivery from evil, *Walam Olum* tells us, the Lenape wandered toward "the rising sun."

The concept of *Manitou* is that of mystery or the supernatural. It can be called the spirit of both good and evil, apparently, but still is said to embody ideas of guardianship, ethical direction, and, perhaps most significantly, cosmic authority. There was an essential oneness to *Manitou*, which leads historians to regard the concept as monotheistic. Despite this, the tribes seemed to admit the reality of certain lesser jinn[1] which were said to inhabit the woods and lesser domains. They were represented by some twelve masks kept in the central structure of the village. Idolatry, however, had virtually no

[1]*A type of spirit capable of appearing in human or animal form.*

place in their beliefs. In fact, so little tangible evidence of their faith did they keep that early Europeans assumed them to have no God.

Actually, much of the religion of the Lenape remains enigmatic, probably because it was passed on traditionally from father to son rather than being recorded. Carved items such as the crude boat-stones, bird-stones, and grooved stones can only be hypothesized as ceremonial items, and, according to Rutgers University experts, their true use may never be determined. It would seem, of course, that like the highly patinated totems worn around the neck, they served a symbolic purpose of some sort. It is known also that the grooved stones could be used as a whistle and the mystical significance of this revelation might have been great to the Indian. Certain other stones were purported to possess medicinal value, and the belief might well have been valuable as a placebo.

Whatever their concrete contribution to the society, the use of carved stones appears a testimonial to the traditions of this early culture, dating back, as some do, at least eight thousand years.

The Dead

All people must at some time reckon with the specter of death, and few indeed are the societies that have not sought the comfort of a belief in an afterlife. The Lenape were no exception, espousing as an adaptation to this need the so-called "Happy Hunting Ground" where the deceased, if worthy, were rewarded for their mortal tribulations by entry into the land of milk and plenty.

The Lenape interred their dead in the flexed position, symbolizing rebirth into the afterlife from an earthy womb. Personal items, utensils, weapons, and even *wampum* were entombed with the body as tokens of affection. One skeleton with a shawl wrapped about his shoulders was found in a Lower Bank cemetery by a Captain Dan Cale. If an individual died during the winter months, when burial was next to impossible, his corpse was often set aside and the flesh allowed to rot from the bones. When warmer weather allowed interment, the skeleton might be transported long distances to its resting place. The Lenape had great affection for their dead. On occasion, when the living group pulled up stakes, they carried the remains with them so that they could keep near the memory of their departed loved ones.

The Life

The sea was of paramount significance to our Indian forebears, so large was its importance that those who controlled the coastal lands had to share them. Inland counterparts would have fought for access to it, but, by treaty, they were allowed to come annually to the shore and draw upon its bounty.

There were five major trails that led toward the Jersey coast. Traveled mainly in spring and autumn, they were narrow — following the path of least resistance — and leading between lookouts and campsites along high ground. One of these was the Manahawkin Trail, that led from Camden along Cooper Creek to Medford, from whence it followed the Bass River to Tuckerton. The Lenape made use of convenient cedar rafts or dugout canoes to reach the sea islands. Dogs, domesticated to an appropriate degree, served as beasts of burden by towing sledges bearing the Indians' belonging.

So it was; each spring, the inland tribes would trek to the sea, eager to harvest again after winter's privations. They came all along the coast, each to a certain traditional locale. Along the Metedeconk River, there are the remains of an early Indian ceremonial place and what is considered to have been a tribal meeting place. Near the headwaters there is a spot, called locally "Paint Island," where flows a spring from which the Indians gathered colored clays and pigments.

There are many such places along the shore, many remaining to this day unexplored. Another such portion of the Barnegat drainage area is a nebulous "Indian Hill," supposedly sloping eastward towards Applegate's Cove. Anticipating hopefully some unusual finds, I sailed down there with a friend in the summer of 1957, making as if it were a clandestine, if belated, forage against the Lenape.

Ascending a gentle slope amongst time-worn pines, which soughed in the southerly, and through clouds of mosquitoes and greenhead flies, we fled, shirt drawn over our heads and arms flailing in vain defense. At the summit, the bulk of our attackers were driven off by the wind and, with inexperienced eyes, I was able to peruse the surroundings. Alas, an occasional oyster shell and the inevitable beer can, but no Indians!

Two years later, I chanced to go ashore at Mosquito Cove,[2] just north of Applegate, on a cut-away beach much frequented by pleasure seekers. Along the regressed face there is a sandy, loam-capped bluff about ten feet high, the base of which just touches the water. Noticing a profusion of shells at one spot along the crumbling rim, I scratched further and revealed what is apparently referred to as the Indian Hill site. Investigation that summer, and in 1960, turned up some artifacts that allowed a narrow and hazy glimpse into early Indian life: the jawbone of a deer, which served its purpose as a scraper for removing corn from the cob; some shards of cheap pottery, which judging by their glaze were pilfered from settlers; the battered remains of a metal knife; what was perhaps a spear tip; the stem of a clay pipe — which, of course, attests to the Indian's addiction to that heinous vice. The volume of shells and occasional lump of charcoal pointed, of course, to the fact that I was dealing with a cooking site. Certain other skeletal remains in the pile proved thankfully to be not those of *Homo sapiens*. I suppose it is only just and objective that I mention the several bricks that my excavations turned up, but as to the significance of those I shall remain conveniently blind. The circumstances, and author Harold Wilson's reference to this place as "Indian Hill," will always people the bluff with Lenape for me.[3]

For those who seek a more thoroughly documented look into the past, I direct all eyes to the *Unami* shell mounds that lie in the marshes south of Tuckerton. If nothing else, they point graphically to the significance of the shore as a source of food. Fish, of course, served in abundance, and even certain seaweeds were of culinary worth, but paramount was the shellfish, which could not flee very effectively and was the source of several useful by-products.

Preparation was, of course, hindered by the animal's shell, held close by the creature's determined adductor muscle. For severance thereof, the Indian developed a little jasper shucking spoon, which was inserted between the valves to release the tenacious grasp. Meats thus obtained were generally smoked and dried on sticks for transportation inland with autumn's onset.

For on-the-spot consumption, the hapless bivalves fared less well. A pit was excavated in the sand, and lined with moist seaweed. The unfortunates, washed clean but quite alive and unsus-

[2] *Known today as Silver Bay.*

[3] *The author revisited this site in 1998. It is now preserved as Ocean County park land. The bank, upon which stabilization has been attempted, is much eroded. I still believe it to be an Indian shell midden. Many diamondback terrapin remains were among the abundant oyster shells.*

pecting, were hurled in and covered with another layer of weed. A good hot fire was ceremoniously kindled on top and upon its expiration, the shellfish steamed to a turn in their own juices. I am told the process will do equally well in these modern times, allowing, of course, that one will never be able to get the same quality of clams you could in "the old days."

Certain of the shells one may find in the Tuckerton mounds bear the mark of an interesting occupation of the shore Indian. They are chipped and rounded mementos of the *wampum* makers.

Wompi

Wampum, deriving from the Algonkian word *wompi*, or white, is no doubt among the most mentioned and least understood products of this aborigine culture. Contrary to popular belief, it was neither money nor currency, and for that matter had in itself no value as a medium of barter. Often it served a symbolic function when woven into belts and was thus employed in the binding of treaties. Its only other value was for personal adornment and, as such it was, actively traded, certain standards of scarcity being set up. The unit of *wampum* was the "fathom,"[4] or distance from the tip of the little finger to the elbow and, needless to say, in such exchanges, the man with a long forearm was at an advantage.

[4] *This is not the mariner's fathom of 6-feet.*

It was only with the arrival of the European that *wampum* began taking on the character of currency. This, appropriately, was a European idea; in the New World, coin was exceedingly scarce and some representative unit was needed to transcend this lack in otherwise cumbersome barter agreements. Convenient *wampum* was introduced at an exchange rate that was geared to the difficulty of its production.

The Dutch were the first to employ the system, setting six white beads equal to a "stiver," one hundred twenty to a guilder, or in English coin, sixpence. On the fathom basis, we are quoted rates of four guilders and five shillings. Some *wampum* belts were twelve or eighteen rows wide and a hundred and eighty beads long, representing countless hours of work and providing a compact local substitute for European coinage. A sad note was sounded for *wampum*, however, when some enterprising chap introduced machine-made beads from the continent. The mechanical productions were probably equal, if not superior, in quality to the originals but naturally the market for both was shortly demolished by sheer currency inflation.

Fabrication of the genuine item was effected by chipping tiny rectangles from the hinge area of an oyster shell. Laboriously each was pierced with a flint drill — which resulted in a discouragingly high rate of breakage — and subsequently rounded into a smooth, uniform bead somewhere around 1/8-inch in diameter. Strung on fibers, they assumed their role of ornamentation.

As implied by the designs frequently evidenced in *wampum* belts, there were forms and colors other than white, which might be considered the "base" of the system. From the leading edge of the northern quahog clam (*Mercenaria mercenaria*) came a small crescent of deep purple shell. Beads fashioned from this were termed "purple" or "black" *wampum* — *suckawhock* to the Lenape — and were assigned a value twice that of white beads. A still more elaborate form came from the valves of the common blue mussel, still found in great profusion along our shores. The bead, as such, was difficult to make owing to the thin, brittle nature of the mussel's valves, but the final product was striking to behold, being jet black on one side and mother-of-pearl on the other. The periwinkle, a small attractive snail of the tidal flats, was also valued by the aborigine and was polished and strung in its natural state.

The Group

For their villages, the Lenape preferred locations bordering on rivers and creeks. Summer dwellers generally lived in tepees that afforded them a degree of mobility not as accessible to permanent residents. The latter used the legendary wigwam, which possibly inspired the versatile Quonset hut of World War II. It was constructed by erecting two parallel rows of saplings which were arched to the center and lashed securely. Subsequently, longitudinal strips were woven basket-like through the uprights and the entirety covered with sedge or grass before being plastered with mud. A door was left at each end for ventilation and access. Another dwelling which may be credited to the Lenape was a primitive variation of the log cabin. Rectangular in shape, it had low, sod-banked walls and an arched roof that was shingled with a relatively waterproof mantle of cedar bark.

The *kingwickaon*, or "big house," was central to each living group and comprised what one might call a meeting place. It contained twelve wooden masks of the lesser deities, suspended from the supporting beams, and was intended thus to placate each deity in the specific domain which he controlled. In times of peace, the wigwams of the tribe might range quite a distance from the *kingwickaon*, but when hostilities threatened, they clustered close, surrounded by a brush palisade.

Land for hunting and cultivation was technically held in common by the tribe. For use, however, it was apportioned, and the land inherited matrilineally. Thus, descent was also traced on the mother's side, following a pattern common to many primitive cultures. By European standards, the men were considered lazy and the women industrious. This followed the traditionally defined roles in their society. The women did domestic chores while men followed the hunting trails and stood in defense of the tribe. Again, by our standards, the women fell far short of an ideal as housekeepers, their huts being as intolerably dirty[5] as the inhabitants.

[5]*But certainly no dirtier than the dwellings of Europeans!*

Monogamy seemed the rule, but since polygamy was permitted, it was practiced only by reason of practicality. The Indian men were no doubt well appraised of "the trouble and annoyance of a plurality of women." The girls were deemed mature at sixteen and consequently donned a crown of bay leaves to signify their availability. The young man reached his maturity about the same age but was required to prove his worth as a brave by performing acts of courage and stamina. On satisfactory performance, he was eligible to take a wife, and a simple ceremony served to bind the two symbolically. The content of the marriage rite seems to vary slightly but the significance is uniform: before suitable witness, the brave handed his bride a piece of meat (or in some localities a bone) and the blushing maid returned to him an ear of corn. With responsibility as to provender set up, little time was lost in establishing a household.

The Warpath

Not all was peaceful with the Lenape even after they conquered the *Allegewi*. The tribes along the north shore of the Mullica had something of a rivalry with the *Unamis* to the south. Once, a party of the former was foraging at some risk in the Leeds Point area. Need I explain that all but one was massacred? The escapee fled, of course, and ended up in the sheltering arms of the Manahawkin tribe. They championed his cause and charged south. They found the victorious *Unamis* and, taking possession of their dugout canoes, killed them to a man. Mulberry Field, where legend places the battle, has always been surprisingly fertile. Mounds nearby, holding the remains of many Indians, were once employed as fertilizer,[6] uncovering many bones and ancient implements. A grisly end to a grisly tale.

[6]*Insensitive as this seems to us now, human bones from European wars were imported to the United States in the 19th century and ground for fertilizer.*

In addition to the customary war-clubs and flint-tipped spears, the Lenape also made use of a five foot long bow, strung with gut. This bow could hurl, with some velocity, a yard-long arrow. The shafts of these arrows were made of light reed, such as grow in our marshes. Despite their origin, if taken from near the root, they are surprisingly rigid and true. A convenient addition, when in battle with fellow *Homo sapiens*, was a weakly fixed flint arrowhead which remained within the flesh as the shaft was withdrawn.

Native Medicinal Practices

While the Lenape of course had numerous herbs to aid in relieving (or perhaps compounding) the sufferings of their ills, they naturally relied very heavily on what would be today termed spiritual healing, or more prosaically, witchcraft. Undoubtedly, however, we must concede that, strengthened by the believing tribesman, the services of the spirit-exorciser were very valuable in the face of such formidable opponents as disease and death. Historians report that the Lenape were most attentive to their sick so long as there was any hope of saving them. On the other hand, they seemed impatient to have the victim either recover or die. Accordingly they adopted what might be termed a "hastening treatment" in which the individual was baked in a hut where water was thrown over red-hot stones. Half-conscious from this, he or she was carried to an icy stream, irrespective of the season, and plunged into its "beneficial" waters.

The newborn, likewise, were strengthened by immersion in a cold stream, winter being preferred for this rite. It served its purpose, no doubt. Surely none but the hardy survived.

The Road of Decline

The arrival of the Europeans brought the Lenape more problems than their society was ultimately able to cope with. As early as 1672 one hears comments from chroniclers that imply decay. One John Burnyeate, in that year, visiting the abode of an "Indian King," reported that he could not offer food nor drink to his guests "so poor was he." On examination, the incident may demonstrate nothing more than Burnyeate's ignorance of the Indians mode of living. Even a chief could hardly offer amenities on a European scale but, in any case, it points out that the Indian lived in balance with his environment, hardly able to waste the fruits of his labor. The white man in Jersey can be said to have upset the balance, if only by displacing the native from the land upon which he depended. The extent of this displacement is graphically illustrated by the fact that, by 1758, most of the Lenape land rights had been bought up. This left only the right to fish in rivers and bays and hunt on those lands that were unenclosed.

In that year, the Lenape became the first tribe of American Indians to be placed on a reservation. The Edge Pillock group was first to succumb, retiring to a 3,044-acre tract near Indian Mills. The basis of the move was said to be an attempt to remove the Indian from the temptation of the white man's vices. The purchase of land rights, however, liberated a lot of territory for profitable development.

Another importation of the Caucasian, one with which the Lenape was wholly unable to cope with was alcohol. Elisha Ashatama, one of the last Lenape in New Jersey, had a fondness for spirits, as illustrated by a local tale. Once, Elisha was offered all the cider he could take home in a basket he was to weave. A member of the Woolman family, who made the proposition, was amazed at the Lenapes resourcefulness when he dipped the basket in a wintry creek and allowed the weave to fuse over with ice. He laboriously lugged off his prize. Drink was, however, to be the end of him, for, in 1833 or 1834, while "graveling" oyster beds in the Mullica, he fell into the water and, being intoxicated, met his death. He was laid to rest in the old Methodist Cemetery at Tuckerton.

The survivors of the "original people" withered slowly on their reservation until 1802 when they enacted a pitiful migration from their beloved ancestral homeland, to New Stockbridge near Lake Oneida, New York. From thence, for one reason or another, they moved again, establishing finally in Statesburgh, on the Fox River in Wisconsin. In 1648, the Lenape numbered nine thousand. In 1832, at Statesburgh, they numbered forty souls.

It was in that year that the survivors elected one of their number, Bartholomew S. "Wilted Grass" Calvin, to represent them before the New Jersey State Legislature in the sale of their few remaining rights. Wilted Grass, who had served in the Revolution under Washington, laid before them his claim, which was met willingly by the government. Wilted Grass returned to his people with $2,000 — the price paid for the birthright of the Lenape.

The last pure Lenape in New Jersey was said to be "Indian Ann," daughter of Elisha Ashatama who, according to folklore, lived in a tepee built by her half-breed son. There she remained, selling baskets, until her death in 1894. Another source says she dwelt in a wigwam, located on the shore road near Barnegat, and still another photographic representation shows a small house in which she was purported to live.

Despite the rather ignominious end suffered by the Lenape, we can point to one deed that remains a credit to the white man. Throughout the colonial and following periods, the controlling government of New Jersey respected the territorial rights of the Indian, invariably compensating him for the loss of his land. Consequently, the state never experienced a major Indian uprising and virtually all difficulties encountered were attributable to personal incompatibilities. This favorable policy was acknowledged by Wilted Grass in his letter to the Legislature following the settlement of 1832:

> Not a drop of our blood have you spilled in battle; not an acre of land have you taken but by our consent. These facts speak for themselves and need no comment. They place the character of New Jersey in bold relief and bright example to those states within whose territorial limits our brethren still remain. Nothing but benisons can fall upon her from the lips of a Lenni Lenape.

The Heritage

Perhaps we cannot maintain that the Lenape left much of a

mathematical legacy, for his system of numbers reached only twenty:

1 - *Cooti*	6 - *Hosh*
2 - *Nishi*	7 - *Cooti-Hosh*
3 - *Nawhaw*	8 - *Hish-Hosh*
4 - *Nayway*	9 - *Pesh-Konk*
5 - *Plainah*	10 - *Tellon*

(11-20 followed the same pattern as 1-9 except that each was prefixed with the number "*Tellon.*" Thus 20 was *Tellon-tellon.*)

We apparently no longer possess a citizen who can speak any of the Lenape dialects but we are told that it was melodic and concise, a single word often expressing three or more English words. William Penn, no doubt in a position to judge, called it "sweet, lofty, and sententious."

Also, the Indian as agriculturalist was no mean producer, for he brought some forty-five wild staple plants under cultivation. The white man, in four hundred years, has a record somewhat less impressive. He hasn't domesticated any.

In a Name

Batsto, in the mind of those historically inclined, immediately conjures the Colonial image of patriots casting cannon balls at the forge of that name but, the word itself dates back somewhat further, to the Lenape *batstoo,* which means "bathing place." This points up a rather significant role of the shore to the Indian, for he enjoyed a swim now and then, too. It was thus at the end of each season, summoned by the phases of the moon, that the Lenape and inland tribes gathered for a last celebration before returning inland for the winter months.

Big Sea Day, as it came to be known, was thus already an established custom when the Indian had vanished. A day was established on the more conventional calendar basis and was formally sanctioned as the second Saturday in August. The event, of course, lost its distinct native character with the entrance of new participants and, while the name Big Sea Day seems to have lasted best, the conclave was called variously Salt Water Day, Beach Day, Farmer's Wash Day, etc.

It was said that one could always tell when it was Big Sea Day because one saw clouds of dust starting up, all at once, in many directions. The farmers came sometimes as far as twenty miles, leaving around noon on Friday and sleeping in their roomy sheet-topped wagons to continue seaward at dawn. They could be seen coming for miles across the coastal plains and through the Pines. Harpers magazine reported 10,000 farmers at a particular Big Sea Day, but maintained that tourists had objected so strongly to the local rowdyism that this represented but a third of former turn-outs.

For many years, the celebration was held at Wreck Pond in Sea Girt. Unfortunately, the romantic name comes not from some ill-fated vessel but what one might consider an anglicization of "Wrack Pond" (for the seaweed accumulating there) or possibly of "Rock Creek," which seems to be the name as early as 1812. A Mr. Larison writes of the festivities there in 1882:

> Thousands from the surrounding country assemble here and have a general wash, and a jolly time. This day is locally styled 'The Sheep Washing Day.' It has been celebrated, I am told, since the earliest times.

Gustav Kobbe, a well known correspondent on the subject, draws moral implications when he states the goings on were at times "unconventional." This, it seems, consisted of the farmers, too poor to purchase legitimate bathing gear, entering the water in their everyday work clothes. Except for drinking, there was nothing more harmful than communal singing at the affair, at least so it is recorded. I have my suspicions otherwise, however, as youth then was, in substance, quite the same as today.

In later years, other attractions began to spring up at Salt Water Day. One chap gathered rattlesnakes in the Pines all year and, assembling them, charged a dime for locals to gape at them. Around 1904, gamblers appeared on the scene, and, with the simple charm destroyed, the locals began losing interest.

However, in 1950, some bright commercial element had "New Jersey's Oldest Festival" revived, this time at Point Pleasant, and with plenty of highly refined money-sponging facilities at hand. At first, one day sufficed, but soon merchants began clambering for a better crack at the crowds. The pageant was extended to three days, and later still a week, allowing the commercial interests a better chance at their victims.

In 1959, it would seem that something of the old informality has been lost in the celebration. On Friday night, the sun is driven from the sky by thunderous fireworks, and the following day a "Miss Seafood Princess" is enthroned to a chorus of popping flash-bulbs and eye balls. The event concludes with a cumbersome, traf-fic-jamming procession, which bellows noisily through the streets. In all fairness, one must admit the affair provides a healthy boost to the local economy and no doubt gives the vast crowds a good time or two. Then again, it is not met with unanimous approval. One local resident, informed of the expanded festivities offered a tacit "oh hell!"

More on names now; this time we turn back south to the Mullica area, this being, as we explained earlier, not an Indian word. Hammonton, we mentioned before, is, stemming from the Lenape name *amintonck*, which was applied to the Mullica in pre-Euro-pean days.

Heading north we come to Manahawkin, from *manna-hock-ing*, which means "good corn land." Near the headwaters of Barne-gat, we find the Metedeconk River, which we are told has gone through metamorphosis from *mittig-conck* to "Muletegung," in 1812, then "Motedeconk," and finally, Metedeconk. The original version supposedly means "place of thrifty woodland," but I have also seen it interpreted as "tall timbers."

Of rather amusing origin is Manasquan,[7] which had its begin-nings in three Lenape words: *man-a-tah* (island — and this is self-evident if one looks at the similarity to "Manhattan"), *squaw* (wife), and *han* (stream). Put together, they come out something like "stream of the island for wives." In explanation, it seems the noble braves left the women there, to keep them in one place and out of harm's way while the men went fishing.

While around the Manasquan River area, we should not forget the tale of "Wills Hole," a slash of deep water cutting southward just inside the inlet.[8] Will, according to one John Tilton of Barne-gat, was quite a man in his day, being stout and broad-shouldered, with prominent Native American features and rings in his nose and ears. Tilton, as a boy in Squan Village, had supposedly culled the observations first hand. Will and "Mrs. Will" lived together in connubial bliss near the water, just about where the old Cook farm

[7] *In my childhood I visited the Manasquan River's lovely island, variously called "Treasure" or "Osborn Island," and have returned several times over the years to lament the increasing load of trash left by careless visitors. Happily, it has been preserved as a park by Monmouth County.*

[8] *This is the channel currently occupied by commercial fishing docks and some restaurants.*

once stood. In bliss, that is, until one night Will's beans weren't done as well as they might have been. He clubbed his unfortunate mate with "a billet of wood" and drowned her in the creek. Shortly, word reached Mrs. Will's two brothers who were Long Island Indians; they soon were on the scene to avenge the deed. Will, being a congenial chap, offered them a drink before they did battle and, when they were thoroughly drunk, knocked them off, too. We are told that he later delighted in telling of his own "revenge." Will's own end came as a bit of appropriate irony, for he drowned one day near the Cook farm.

Local history maintains that Toms River takes its name from one Thomas Pumha, otherwise known as "Indian Tom" or "Barnegat Tom." Tom was a son of Popomera, a chief of the Navesinks and lord of many acres. By his birthright he was chief of the Metedeconks. A map drawn in 1740 shows a "Barnegat Tom's Wigwam" located on an island north of Mosquito Cove, probably what is today Green Island. Again, local sources say he dwelt for many years around the time of the Revolution at Money Island, just west of Long Point in Toms River. As the two sources cover different periods of time, we can perhaps consider them as complementary.

While at Money Island, Tom apparently rendered services to the Patriot cause and received the honor of having "Goose Creek," as it was called in the early part of the century, renamed "Tom's River." General recognition was, however, not obtained until after 1777, for "Goose Creek" still persisted in that year. Well, it's a nice tale, but if we don't stop there, we will find "Tom's River" on a map prior to 1727. This rather demolishes the "Indian" Tom legend, so, whence cometh the name?

Captain William Tom, a young surveyor along the Delaware, pushed eastward to the Atlantic, we are told, in the year 1684. According to a Toms River tourist publication, *The Guidepost*, some sixteen families settled that very year along Captain Tom's picturesque river, with its sandy bluffs and coastal surroundings. Although the settlement bore no name as yet, it became the first village in Ocean County and one of the first ten European habitations on the continent of North America.[9]

During his earlier years along the Delaware, Captain Tom had entered the service of the Crown from 1665 to 1675, and was

[9]*This can't be accurate, considering the long-established Spanish New World settlements, the Canadian Maritimes, the several colonies of the Chesapeake, North Carolina, New England and New York!*

considered by the British to be "the most useful man alive." Such would seem to validate his claim to "Tom's River," and so it remained until the 1880s, when the apostrophe, that denoter of the possessive, was lost to the past and it became simply "Toms River."[10]

Whether one espouses the claims of William Tom or Indian Tom, we owe the Indian a large debt of heritage. However, fortunately or otherwise, the white man seems to have come out on top, so let us turn to a consideration of the victor, to whom went the spoils of *Scheyechbi.*

Chapter 6

The Fate of
Scheyechbi

Post-Exploratory European Occupations

Both Hendrik Hudson and Cornelius Mey flew the
Nederlandische flag, and so our hallowed region fell
first into Dutch hands about 1617, when a few drove
property line stakes in New Jersey at what is today
Bergen County. New Jersey as a whole held little lure for the Netherlands; thus, when another West India company was organized in
1621, they built their fort at "New Amsterdam," site of present-
day New York. The company's endeavors in building the colony of
New Netherlands concentrated mainly on trading. Difficulties with
the Indians made farming on the few small and far-flung farms
less than secure. Thus, from their log palisade on Manhattan, the
staid Hollanders viewed *Scheyechbi's* highlands looming dully
through blue mists across the Hudson.

Simultaneously, the ubiquitous British were not to be outdone.
James I signed a charter in 1606, ceding to the Plymouth Trading
Company the Atlantic coast between the Delaware Bay and Port
Royal. Isham, in *The Fishery Question,* notes that this was done
"without knowledge of the geography of the country," and no doubt

without regard to its ownership.

Working on the basis of this precedent, Charles II, in March of 1664, closed his eyes to the established Dutch Colony and granted New Jersey, New York, and Connecticut jointly to his beloved brother James, Duke of York, and one Richard Nicolls. Obviously it wasn't quite that simple and accordingly, the next spring, Nicolls fitted out a fleet and sailed over to claim his prize. In April, his ships lay in the Hudson tide with gunports gaping and the threat of iron broadsides leveled on poor little New Amsterdam.

Faced with a military ultimatum, a bellicose Peter Stuyvesant stumped out on his wooden leg on April 17, 1665, and surrendered to the English.

The Duke of York, meanwhile, proceeded to deed out his acquisition. Among other grants, he delegated those lands south of 41°, 40' north latitude to Lord Berkeley and Sir George Carteret, former governor of the British Isle of Jersey; the lands delineated in the so-called "Monmouth Patent" were to be titled *Nova Caesaria*. For one reason or another, Berkeley lost his grip on things in March, 1673 and sold his holdings to two Quaker gentlemen, John Fenwick and Edward Byllings. The two Friends, undoubtedly satisfied with their purchase, must have been a bit shaken when, a brief four months later in July, 1673, the Dutch recaptured New York.

As fate would have it, *Nova Caesaria* again changed hands in 1674, when a treaty was negotiated, ceding her for a second time to the English. A struggle ensued to readjust land titles as they existed under the original "Nicolls Patent." Fenwick and Byllings had originally hoped that Jersey would be completely free, both politically and religiously. They themselves, however, fell to quarreling over deeds, and their holdings came eventually into the hands of another Quaker, William Penn, and his associates, late in the 1670s. Despite this, the conflict was less than settled and, accordingly, the Colony was divided into East and West Jersey, as determined by a line running from Old Inlet, at a point near Bonds on the sea beach, to Rankokus Kill, a point along the Delaware at 41° north latitude. Designed as a device for simplifying titles, the line served only to compound difficulties in later years when, as explained earlier, the inlet shifted. But, aside from its purported socially propitiating effects, it produced some decent maps of the area, such as Worlidge's, which appeared in 1700.

The division became legal on July 1, 1676, when a "Quint-ipartite Deed" was executed by Carteret, William Penn, *et al.* As is apparent, this left virtually all the Barnegat Bay area under East Jersey, led by the capricious Sir George Carteret, with such dissensions present that the region was shortly ceded to the Crown.

In 1702, Queen Anne, the then-reigning monarch, reunited the Jerseys, giving them the right to self-administration as a Royal Province in 1708. Lord Cornbury was chosen first Governor by Her Majesty, and he was assisted by the Surveyor General of West Jersey, Daniel Leeds.

Enter, the Relatives

This, I say with reservations, for I claim kinship by only the most tenuous thread of an uncle by marriage, on my father's side. He (Clarence Merideth Leeds) traced a direct male line to Daniel Leeds.

Born in Leeds, England in 1652, Daniel Leeds brought his family to the new colony in 1676, settling in Shrewsbury, near Perth Amboy (then Sweet Perth Town), which was the seat of government. The rule of Colonial Governor Lord Cornbury seems to have been wholly corrupt and strongly opposed by the people. In an attempt to save their vested interests, Leeds and an accomplice named Revell petitioned Queen Anne to redress grievances against the governor. The people, however, protested so generally and vigorously that a new appointee, Governor Lovelace was installed on April 19, 1708.

Leeds, meanwhile, had established himself well in South Jersey, taking to his bosom Leeds Point, which, with the aid of his son, Japeth, he had surveyed and settled. Appropriately, it was the highest point of land between the Highlands and the Virginia Capes. Mr. Leeds, anticipating *Poor Richard* by a good many years, published a popular almanac from 1687 until 1717. He died peacefully in 1720, and was interred at Shrewsbury.

The Populace

When England assumed control of the Jerseys in 1674 for the last time, they, unlike the Dutch, instituted a relatively liberal government, which was conducive to settlers. Most of the earlier arrivals were New Englanders, spreading out along the coast in search of whaling grounds. They found what they were looking for off the Jersey coast. However, the ownership, especially in West Jersey, was predominantly Quaker. Shortly, the Quaker element, spreading eastward, was to overbalance the population. The two groups were not at odds and co-existed well during this period.

By and large however, the Barnegat Bay area remained largely unpopulated until the 18th century. We spoke of William Tom in the previous chapter, and his purported colonization of the Toms River area around 1684. This is the first evidence we have of people settling in the region attributed to a specific year.

In 1696, Hendrick Jacobs Falkinburg (or Falconbre) arrived at Tuckerton from Delaware's Quaker colony to the west. Circa 1700, several families came to key points along the bay.

Jacob Ong joined the Falkinburgs at Tuckerton in 1698, Thomas Tow was at Barnegat by 1720 and the noted Cranmers[1] were in town by 1729.

Still, we can hardly call development along the coast a building boom, for in 1770, Thomas Potter is quoted as saying there were only seven hundred people in twenty miles along the shore. Six years later, Tuckerton was the largest village on the coast, being a legal port of entry. Japeth Leeds, in the interim, had a grandson named Jeremiah, who, growing up along the shore, was familiar with its nascent shipping centers. All were to figure greatly in the Revolution when Jerseymen became a thorn in the side of Governor William Franklin — and a thorn in the Crown of England.

Such, friends, was the fate of *Scheyechbi*.

[1] *The Cranmers, expatriate descendants of Archbishop Cranmer, who fared poorly in English politics, are still very much in New Jersey.*

Chapter 7

A Thorn for
The Crown

The Conflict

George III of England had a state crown, well supplied with jewels but, as it turned out, he also had a crown of thorns; thirteen thorns for thirteen colonies, one of which was *Nova Caesaria*. Stripped of patriotic and philosophical considerations, the American "colonial rebellion" was basically the result of poor management. England believed that since she was a manufacturing nation, the colonies should exist for her support by supplying raw materials for fabrication in the mother country. This was clearly to the benefit of British merchants and to the detriment of colonial initiative. Reality dictates that the great majority of colonists came to the new world in search of personal gain or escape from restriction. Plainly, they were a bunch of radicals who wanted their own way.

Actually, the above is an oversimplification of the uprising. The Navigation Acts, so often extolled as a prime injustice, had been in effect for some time. By and large the colonists settled in full awareness of them, and in awareness that they were far less strict than in other Crown colonies. Likewise, the trade restrictions were somewhat less crippling than many would have us believe. No one liked them, to be sure, but people learned to smuggle around them quite well, and smuggling was somewhat more profitable than free trade.

Gunpowder in the Leaves

Real trouble came, surprisingly, with a momentary relaxation of stiff tariffs imposed on tea entering the colonies directly - without being handled through English ports (and merchants) first. When British East India Company ships began bringing tea directly to American ports, the market for expensive smuggled Dutch tea went flat, and the smugglers howled fiercely. The colonial rowdyism that sprang from this situation consisted mostly of reprisals on their Tory fellow colonists.

Focusing a moment on New Jersey, we find that, early in colonial times, when tea was introduced, few of our citizens knew what it was for! Some housewives boiled it for several hours, threw out the tea and served the dregs with butter and salt as "greens." Apparently, they liked it this way, or perhaps their mistaken impressions were corrected, for later in the period they held a tea party of their own, burning an English shipment of tea at Greenwich on the Delaware Bay in Cumberland County.

Most Americans were shocked by the activities of their fellows, but not so much as Parliament, which proceeded to pass the "Intolerable Acts." Shortly thereafter, the individualistic ire of our leading gentlemen was aroused and the First Continental Congress was convened. They set a flat ultimatum before the Crown: repeal these laws or fight. Unfortunately, thousands of miles separated the two groups in mind and thought and, accordingly, on July 4, 1776, the Declaration of Independence was issued. Those fleeting shots fired in New England on April 19 the year before had become the American Revolution.

New Jersey has been called the "Cockpit of the Revolution" because so many armies crossed her soil. Only a few decisive battles took place within her boundaries and even these were outside today's Ocean County which comprises much of the Barnegat Bay area. Yet the bay and her surroundings were critical in many ways to the cause: as a backwater, they formed a relatively secure base for moving supplies. The British full realized this, and the tense dramas the situation engendered certainly bear telling.

Barnegat Pirates

Prominent in the struggle were the depredations of the "Pine Woods Robbers" who, acting under the guise of being Royalists, stole indiscriminately from Tory and Patriot alike. It would be unjust however, in our consideration of the fleeing Royalist refugees (or simply "refugees," as they were also known) to class all of them with the pine robbers; many, perhaps most, were deeply convinced of their cause. Their units composed the New Jersey Royalist volunteers. Further, we can hardly vindicate all the actions of the so-called patriots, since many took advantage of the situation so as to become nothing more than pirates themselves.

As seems often the case in human affairs, the neutral was placed in a rather precarious position. Under threats of reprisal he was bound to house and under like, if more informal, threat, he had to fulfill an obligation to his own local militia. The story is told of a family who was in the midst of fulfilling its Loyalist obligations by feeding the Loyalist volunteers when a band of hungry locals arrived on the scene. The table was rapidly cleared and a new repast spread for the comers. When they had finished, the unsympathetic Royalists emerged to demand the balance of their meal.

In Chapter 4, we noted the privateering activities that originated out of Toms River during the conflict. If we, as Americans, are to make a distinction between piracy and privateering, perhaps the most convenient, though not necessarily just, line to draw is between Tory and Patriot. Admittedly, the line between piracy and patriotism that these men sailed was a thin one, and probably few are the men who did not transgress its bounds at one point in their career. Nevertheless, we cannot avoid bias toward our own cause, and perhaps, in a sense, we are justified in not trying.

If we look at the situation around the upper bay, near the foot of what today comprises Monmouth County, we encounter the charming personage of Royalist Jacob Fagan. Fagan worked, we are told, in the Bay Head area, foraging out from his hidden cave on what later became the George Patterson farm in Ardena. The location was commemorated by titling the place "Fagan Cave Farm." The remains of the hideout might still be found if one were diligent, and there is supposedly buried treasure in the area (isn't there everywhere?). The trees, however, that once screened the spot from view have long since vanished, and with them went what might have been a clue to the location.

Fagan and his boys once attacked the home of a neighbor, Major Dennis, who subsequently took his family away, building a new home on the Shrewsbury River. Fagan, the dog, followed soon after with the intent of further plunder. He was shot in ambush and, after managing to crawl away, died in the woods. Soldiers found his body and buried it, but angered locals exhumed it for "appropriate" mutilation. It was hung in a tree about a mile from Colt's Neck, wrapped in chains and tarcloth, and left to rot before the winds. Buzzing with insects it fell bone by bone to the earth. Finally, someone spiked the skull to the tree with a pipe in its mouth, a silent reminder to those who would follow in his footsteps. In all, the treatment seems a bit gross. Rationality is rarely a part of such affairs, and it is well to note that at least they waited until Fagan was dead before desecrating his body.

A stream leading into the main flow of Toms River just above the town proper bears the name Davenport Branch after another ignoble Revolutionary figure. The Davenport gang gained some notoriety in the Toms River area by means of their depredations upon the Patriots. On June 1, 1782, they put out from Forked River in two long barges, each bearing about forty men. About half the group was white and the balance composed of black "picaroons," or escaped slaves. Bent on plunder, the barges parted ways, one heading north toward the salt works on Goose creek above Toms River and the other south towards Waretown. The latter's approach went not unnoticed by the Waretown militia who came out to engage the invaders with a small swivel cannon. One of the balls neatly smacked into Davenport, killing him instantly. Other shots damaged the barge, which the activity of its men soon capsized, into about four feet of water. Prodded by Patriot musketry, and no doubt the sight of their leader so finally dispatched, they fled through the muck and managed to gain the cover of an along-shore cedar swamp. Here they hid for some time before disbanding to flee the country, begging their way along on the charity of Quaker farmers.

What happened to the other barge? We are told that somewhere around this time the Coates' Point Works (bordering Goose Creek on the north) were burned, but there is apparently no record that it was connected with the Davenport forage of June 1.

Still at Toms River, we note Goodluck Point, a low marshy promontory on the southern side of the river's mouth, studded today by a forest of telegraph poles which comprise the above-ground portion of a giant antenna. American Telephone and Telegraph (AT&T) had a radio station there in the late 1920s, a key point in the development of signal transmission.[1] Presently it serves local boatmen with appropriately timed weather information, broadcast on 2558 K.C. on WAQ. The name, however, harks back once more to the Revolution, and one of the fleeing refugees named McMullen who, pursued hotly by the local militia, came up on the north shore of the river. There was a swirling tide, bound seaward toward Cranberry Inlet. Having little choice in the matter, he spurred his mount into the water, and, after an exhausting swim, gained the opposite bank. He turned toward his distant pursuers and, waving his hat, shouted: "Good luck! Good luck!" The militia agreed he had had good luck, and the name stuck.

[1] NOAA's national weather broadcasts assumed this role later in the 20th century.

Island Beach, uninhabited during the conflict period, served as an ideal base for some of the less revered Loyalists. Among them was a Captain John Bacon, who purportedly based some of his raids from a spot amongst the dunes south of Cranberry. He is also said to have operated from certain cedar swamps near Goodluck Point and to have imperiled the area from Cedar Creek south to Parkertown. Certainly Bacon scribed his name to the role of infamy one night on Long Beach Island.

On October 25, 1782, a cutter out of Ostend, Belgium, bound for St. Thomas grounded on the shoals off Barnegat Inlet. An American privateer galley, the *Alligator*, discovered her there, and being advised that she was loaded with valuable, and scarce, Hyson tea, they notified Patriots ashore who soon appeared on Long Beach Island with the intent of salvaging the cargo. The group of twenty-five was headed by Captain Steelman of Cape May and was composed of locals from the Waretown-Tuckerton area. They worked nearly all day hauling in the cased tea before camping exhausted amongst the dunes at dusk. The spot was no more than a mile below Barnegat Inlet, or so it was reported by later sources. At any rate, "Barnegat Shoals" were involved, according to a New York Tory newspaper, which wrote up the incident a few days later.

Meanwhile, a survivor of the cutter had reached John Bacon

and his band, who naturally had a similar interest in the valuable prize. Captain Bacon immediately set out across Barnegat Bay in a small sloop, which legend informs us was named the *Hero's Revenge*. Secreting their craft along the marsh, he and his men crept up the dunes and surrounded the sleeping and unsuspecting party. Without quarter, they opened fire and in a few moments had killed twelve of the Patriots. Only five managed to flee unharmed and the balance carried scars of the incident to their graves.

The surrounding counties were enraged by the Long Beach Massacre and, subsequently, a reward of fifty pounds sterling was posted for Bacon's capture or assassination. His pillages, however, continued until one day he was spotted in John Rose's tavern, which was between Tuckerton and West Creek. Enter the avengers. The day was April 3, 1783; the Revolution was technically over, but memories of Long Beach did not fade so easily.

Bacon attempted to escape but was bayoneted by William Cooke; he fell wounded to the floor. Captain John Stewart took charge of the prisoner and posted Cooke on guard outside the door. Bacon, realizing his only hope of survival was escape, staggered to his feet and made for the door. Cooke heard the commotion and turned towards the building. At that moment Stewart fired his rifle point blank. The bullet passed through Bacon, killing him instantly, shattered the doorjamb and hit poor Cooke in the breast. While Stewart had ended John Bacon's career with irrevocable finality, it was ironic that the very bullet that killed him, avenged his bayonet wound by also hitting Cooke, though apparently Cooke received only a superficial injury from the spent bullet.

Bacon could hardly have been popular under the circumstances, for some of the group were close relatives of men who had died the October before on the sea-beach. According to English custom, he was in the process of being buried beneath a public highway, when his brother came on the scene and begged to take the body away for a decent burial. The men of Jacobstown had their fill of blood, and granted the request.

If we must analyze John Bacon, the man, it would seem that he was a product of the times. He was fighting for a cause, and legitimately so, as were many of his fellow colonials. When one sees the reasons for which people side in our present political campaigns, there is little room for self-righteous criticism. Only in light of the Long Beach massacre could we question his basic humanity, and, indeed all the facets of this affair will never be revealed.

Dick Bird was another who espoused the Crown cause, as far as we can determine. He hailed originally from Potters Creek at what is presently Bayville, but during the Revolution he took to dwelling in a cave that was excavated from the bank of Cedar Creek. Dick had a girl, and was visiting her one evening as was his custom, in her cabin located near Quail Run. Local women spotted him on the way to his tryst. They notified the militia, who surrounded the place. Dick, though engrossed with the lady who was ensconced on his lap, noticed a face fleeting past the window and leapt for his gun, which was standing by the chimney. As his hand closed over the stock, a Patriot bullet ended this bid for freedom. The legend further tells that the lady was going through his clothes and pockets even before his slayers had entered the cabin. Perhaps she had already earned her fee and was seeking collection before intervention would relieve her of her due.

Another Tory, Bill Giberson, had a sister who was as much a man as he was. It is said she could jump, standing, from one hogshead[2] to another, alongside, without touching the sides of either! Bill, we are told, with a running start, could clear an Egg Harbor wagon. Despite his jumping prowess, Bill was captured early one morning by Benjamin Bates near Manahawkin. Bill distracted him on the way to jail and managed to escape. The next day, on a hunch, Ben Bates returned to Giberson's cabin and waited for him. Sure enough, he came on the scene, just as Ben was cautiously entering through the door. Ben's only clue to this was the sound of a musket being cocked. Instinctively, he dropped to his knees, and the ball passed through his hat. Spinning, he shattered the fleeing Giberson's leg, and this time the wounded man was locked in a Mount Holly jail.

Despite the efforts of colonial medicine, Bill's leg healed well enough for him to get around. Before long, his sister came on the scene in her wagon for a visit. It's a testimony to her resemblance to Bill that the jailer helped him get "his" skirts into the wagon most courteously before he drove away. Perhaps it was sheer amazement, or lack of proper facilities, but Bill's sister went free too, and the pair left secretly for New York. Bill later went to Nova Scotia,

[2] *A large cask or barrel.*

as did many Tories after the Revolution. In several years, he returned to live at peace with his former adversaries, settling in Atlantic County.

Still another Tory, Joseph Mulliner, followed a rather traditional pattern, at least according to legend, pilfering from the rich and — sometimes — giving to the poor. A favorite trick was having one of his boys, "Big Dan" Johnson, cry out for aid in a shrill voice, waylaying the Samaritans when they came to answer. A preferred target for such doings were the provision wagons of Batsto Forge, which could be conveniently driven away. Some questionably more fortunate of the Batsto teamsters were sold protection against such eventualities, perhaps in an 18th century version of organized crime.

Joe was something of a master at camouflaged troop movement. He had his band sit astride cedar logs, resplendent with foliage, and paddle them along the wooded shores of the Mullica, which was his stomping ground. He was considered a cool character, and one meticulous in dress and speech. He maintained a uniform, along with a huge sword and a brace of pistols. The rifle he carried was said to be over 6-feet long. He had a dog, which acted as messenger for the band of refugees his master headed. Despite his occasional generosity, Joe is said to have gained a reputation for many bloodthirsty acts. However, his crowning injustice seems to be the rape of a Miss Honore Read, whose father was an ironmaster in the area. We are not told how this event tied in with the woman to whom Joe was supposedly married; at any rate, locals tracked him to his den in a hemlock swamp north of Batsto. Camouflage did him no good then.

Captured and sentenced, Joe was brought up beneath a towering birch tree outside Burlington, in his own wagon. Thousands gathered for the spectacle, and heard Mulliner make a passionate confession of his sins and state the justice of his sentence. There on "Gallows Hill" he jiggled and gasped out his end on August 16, 1781, and was buried without ceremony. His wife moved the remains to Pleasant Mills, where they rested until 1860, when some drunken woodcutters dug up the bones and took them to Batsto. A court order later returned them to the original resting place.

Joe's soul did not rest, be it from the burden of his deeds, or mere concern over the booty he left behind, and each spring he is seen to float amongst the mists along the Mullica. A wooden sign remained into the 20th century, marking the tree where he died.

Trackdown

Mulliner, Fagan, Davenport, and Bacon shared the final fate of many Royalists hunted down in the last days of the Revolution. Others were able to follow the example of Giberson and flee from Monmouth and Ocean counties to the safety of Nova Scotia. Under the circumstances, they were probably wisest in this course, for conditions in America were far from stable for some time after the conflict ended. Absenting themselves between 1782 and 1783 allowed many former Tories to return peaceably to their homes and later resume a reasonable existence.

The Privateers

Jeremiah Leeds, Japeth's grandson, grew into a powerful man, six foot tall and weighing around 250-pounds. Such was his stamina that at age sixty-two, he married a twenty-four year old girl named Milly Ingersoll. Before his demise she bore him four children.

When Jeremiah was still young, he and his brother purchased some steers, which they grazed on the beaches after local custom. One morning, while Jeremiah's father was in the area, a British man o' war put a boat full of soldiers ashore and took two head from the herd. His father, noting discretion to be the better part of valor, left them to their work. They were his sons' steer, after all. As steers were worth five or six dollars a head then, the boys took it less lightly and immediately set off to war. For such cause was a privateer born, and Jeremiah operated out of Egg Harbor, along with his fellows, throughout the war years.

By 1779, Captain Joseph Sooy, of an old bay family, was operating his commissioned privateer schooner *Prosperity* in the area. He brought his prize ships to port, for sale under the Admiralty court of New Jersey, presided over by Marshall Joseph Potts. Naturally, the British were at odds with such goings on, for nightly from that nest of Rebel pirates came swift boats to overwhelm vessels of superior size and armament. It is said that as many as

³A cat-schooner with
the foremast raked
sharply to the bow.

thirty armed sloops and pirogue³ often lay in wait for victims off
the shoals:

> Friday last, Captain Wedham arrived here from Providence.
> Last Sunday he was chased by a schooner privateer from Egg Har-
> bor as far to the Eastward as Martha's Vineyard.

The Battle of Chestnut Neck

Along with the important role of privateering, which made our
coast one of the most critical points on the seaboard, the bog-iron
forges were turning out tons of cast iron shot for the Continental
Army.

⁴The original name
for Tuckerton.

Thus by 1778, the English commanders had had quite enough
of the boys from Chestnut Neck, Egg Harbor Meeting House,
and Clamtown⁴, while the Redcoats inland equally had had their
fill of Gloucester iron. They resolved to take action.

Inside Old Inlet, an attack had been anticipated long in ad-
vance. The year 1777 saw a small fort with sand embrasures erected
by Colonel Elijah Clark and Colonel Richard Wescott at Fox Burrows, a point overlooking the Mullica at Chestnut Neck. The two
officers used their own money until the Continental Congress voted
them an appropriation. The sum of forty-three pounds, one shil-
ling, three pence went to John Cox at Gloucester Forge in Batsto
for the purchase of two dozen iron cannon. Of the first dozen,
delivered in 1776, three blew up on the first shot. Cox altered his
efforts accordingly and of the next dozen five exploded. The failure, according to local sages, was laid to the softness of the bog
iron, which they maintained was inferior to the inland breed. The
WPA (Works Progress Administration), dredging the channel off
Samuel Frenche's place in the 1930s, came up with one of these
guns.

At any rate, Egg Harbor kept functioning, still without reprisal,
and through the winter of 1778, supplied the desperately crippled
troops at Valley Forge. Merchant vessels discharged their cargoes
to flat boats in Egg Harbor by which they were conveyed westward to the "forks" where the river became unnavigable. Here,
supplies were moved over sand roads by wagon and boated across
the Delaware. This chain literally kept Washington alive, and may

well have been said to have preserved the Revolution.

It was in August, 1778, that the merchantman *Venus* passed Egg Harbor shoals on her way to New York from London laden with silks, silver, and tons of general cargo ranging from guns to watchsprings. Captain Micaja Stevens in the schooner *Sly* and Captain David Stevens in the *Chance* moved over the bar in pursuit.

Ships in those days carried several guns under the transom, called "stern chasers." They gave a vessel fire power against following vessels. As long as these guns could be used, the pursuers had a rough time beating up alongside to engage, for with chain and grape-shot her decks could be swept clear. However, fate was not aboard the *Venus* that day. She had hardly begun her flight when one of her heavy guns aft exploded, killing the mate and some of the crew. The captain was rattled by the event, and struck his colors to the privateers. Shortly thereafter, the *Major Pearson* was also taken, and both ships were sailed as prizes into Egg Harbor. These were the not-so-diminutive straws that broke the British patience, for in the last week of September, 1778, Sir Henry Clinton gathered a task fleet in New York Harbor.

Four armed galleys were ordered out, as were the sloops *Vigilant, Nautilus,* and the *Zebra,* commanded by Captain Henry Collins. The *Zebra* sailed as flagship and aboard her was Captain Patrick "Scotch" Ferguson, in command of a military arm composed of three hundred foot soldiers from the British Fifth Regiment and one hundred or more Third Batallion New Jersey volunteers. On September 30, the ships slid out of New York Harbor and a patriot rider raced south to warn the colonists at Egg Harbor.

Immediately, preparations began in anticipation of the coming holocaust. Three well-armed prizes and a pilot boat with guns were sent to sea where they would be clear of harm. Several other craft were scuttled, as crews to man them at sea could not be spared. At Batsto, the iron molders hid their unfinished shot in the depths of Mordecai Swamp. Not much was recovered, but since then, some has turned up in the muck. On October 7, 1778, Ferguson's force appeared off Old Inlet and the last few ships were hastily rushed upriver to Chestnut Neck where it was hoped they would escape molestation.

Captain Ferguson took the opportunity to seize an American

fisherman, Nathaniel Cowperthwaite, as pilot for the tricky passage inside. Nathaniel delayed until dark, and, in the interim, he cleverly managed to run aground the armed sloops *Granby* and *Greenwich*. With the night, he slipped overboard and swam ashore.

The delay was well advised, for the morning of the seventh brought winds, and the larger ships found it impossible to enter the harbor. Ferguson decided to act anyway and loaded his troops into some of the smaller craft. They proceeded across Great Bay and up the Mullica, destroying two already scuttled prizes and setting to the torch eight sloops, schooners, and pirogues, which were in high demand as swift privateers. Chestnut Neck and the pitiful fortifications at Fox Burrows were demolished. The captain later advised his superiors:

> Brig of 16, sloop of 12, schooner of 8, and pilot boat of 6 guns brought over the bar and are at Fox Burrows in possession of a brig. Several vessels are expected hourly.

It was his intention to continue inland to the Forks, where Batsto might be destroyed. He decided against it, and, near sunrise on October 7, moved back toward his ships, smashing three salt works and wrecking the home of Eli Mathis despite a banquet then in progress. No doubt sour grapes from the tired and hungry Redcoats! At daybreak, Ferguson was dismayed to find that both the *Zebra* and the *Vigilant* had come aground on the bar in an attempt to enter Egg Harbor. He worked with his men all that day and half the following night trying to free them. The *Vigilant* was finally liberated but the *Zebra* was to remain fast. Throughout the following week, Ferguson ravaged the area, softening it up, it would appear, for a lunge at the Egg Harbor Meeting House, which was a reputed hangout for local privateers. Remains from some of the troop barges used by the attackers were still visible at low water in the 1880s, lying just where they had been abandoned.

To the Rescue

On October 5, 1778, the famed *Pennsylvania Packet* published an announcement of the arrival of General Pulaski's legion of horse and foot, to join General Washington's command. Pulaski was immediately notified of the situation at Egg Harbor and commenced a forced march overland to the scene. It was probably late Wednesday, October 7, that he entrenched his men as a buffer between the British and Little Egg Harbor Meeting House. His three companies of light infantry and three troops of light horse and volunteers were quartered October 8 on James Willet's farm, from where the supposedly stymied British force could be observed. A half mile down the island road, where the ground leveled out towards the saltmarsh, Lt. Colonel Baron DeBosen was established with forty-some men as a picket post.

Lieutenant Gustav Juliet, an arrogant officer under DeBosen, took five of the men fishing in a punt during the night of October 13. He discreetly passed the bottle under guise of friendship and, getting three of the men drunk, turned them all over to Ferguson. He falsely informed the British commander that Pulaski had issued a no-quarter order against the British in the event the two forces should engage. Ferguson, of course, was enraged, and he proposed revenge for such an order. DeBosen, meanwhile, not sensing the magnitude of the situation, was glad to be relieved of the brazen Juliet.

Near midnight on October 14, Juliet guided Ferguson and a party of two or three hundred men as they swept in with the tide towards Osborn Island. Here they captured the Quaker homestead of Richard Osborn, demanding that they be guided to DeBosen's outpost. Thomas, Richard's son, was forced into the heinous role at sword's point, and with muffled oars the boats slid up a rancid cedar creek, just at peak tide. The dozing sentry was surprised, and silently the raiders entered the camp.

Muskets blasted into the half-sleeping defenders; many were killed with their pants only partway on. DeBosen rushed down the farmhouse stairs, sword in one hand, pistol in the other, but a regular ran him through, on Juliet's order, before he could use either. In a few moments, forty men lay dead beneath a drifting blur of gunsmoke and five were dragged, stumbling, off into the night, as the invaders beat a hasty retreat. No cry for quarter had been heeded.

Young Osborn stood dazedly amongst the trees, shaken to the very core by what his young eyes had witnessed. He was still there when, but a few minutes later, Pulaski's men burst into the yard. Dazed at first by the bloody sight, they soon marshaled a pursuit through the still-lingering haze of pungent sulfur and nitrates. But the British had laid their plan carefully. In retreating, they crossed a tide-swollen creek, methodically ripping the planks off the bridge deck behind them. The bulk of Pulaski's men were thus delayed, and Ferguson escaped all but sniper chastisement. He returned to the *Zebra*, which had by then been re-floated.

In the interim, some of Pulaski's troopers had wandered about the gory scene on Willet's farm. Horrified by the heartless massacre of their fellows, and frustrated in revenging it, they seized poor Osborn, who had stumbled among them, and bound him to a tree. He was slapped around and called a Tory and a Quaker coward, and threatened with a brutal demise until officers, returning from the abortive chase, put him in protective custody. The traditional scapegoat had been saved.

The gray of dawn found Colonel Thomas Procter of the Continental Army approaching with Count Pulaski's detachment of light artillery, and a heavy brass field piece bouncing along behind. The approach of gunnery that the British were not prepared to meet prompted Ferguson to order retreat on July 15, but, as the ill-fated *Zebra* passed over the bar on her way to sea, she struck hard again. Captain Collins ordered her debarked to the other vessels, and, when she could not be floated, put her to the torch.

It was with satisfied smiles indeed that Egg Harbor privateers greeted the "shotted guns...heard to discharge when flames enveloped the vessel." Scotch Ferguson, meanwhile, crammed aboard one of the smaller vessels, reflected on the events past in a report to his superior:

> We had an Opportunity of destroying part of the Baggage and Equipment of Pulaski's legion by burning their Quarters, but as the house belonged to some inoffensive Quakers, who I am afraid, may have sufficiently suffered already in the confusion of a night's scramble, I know Sir, that you will think with us, that the Injury to be thereby done to the enemy would not have compensated for the sufferings of these Innocent People.

While I'm sure that Pulaski could hardly muster our objectivity, we must look upon Ferguson as a decent man. His actions on the night of October 14, 1778, followed only what he believed to be justice. Juliet, legend records, will be forever doomed to fish at night at the spot where he betrayed his fellows.

The battle left little behind, except its dead, to recall the incident. Chestnut Neck was burned to the ground and her residents, mostly women, children, and those too old or feeble to fight, picked up their belongings and rebuilt up Nacote Creek. The Franklyn Inn, in Port Republic, was built by Daniel Mathis with scraps he picked up following the conflagration. Of the British vessel *Venus*, which in large measure precipitated the events, Henry Charlton Beck reports that some children chased chickens off an old capstan bar in Port Republic that bore her name. That, and the blackened sheave of one of her blocks, is all that has been recovered. In a nebulous tavern "up the road to New York,[5]" we are told that tankards and pewter mugs from the *Zebra* were used occasionally for beer, even into this century.

[5]*Route 9 was called the New York Road before highways were numbered.*

But perhaps of greatest significance was the fact that in the few weeks following the Battle of Chestnut Neck, Little Egg Harbor was as much a thorn to British merchantmen as it had ever been.

The Role of Toms River

Toms River, too, was a critical supply route for the embattled colonies. Square riggers entering Cranberry Inlet filled many a sheet-topped wagon with goods that subsequently trundled hastily to waiting troops in the interior. But, thanks to that very inlet, the town was more than a seaport. On Coates Point, on the north shore of the river itself, were located government subsidized salt works, engaged in extracting that critical commodity from the sea.[6] It was, of course, the most basic of condiments, but also a necessary preservative for food, both on land and at sea, and was a factor in the manufacture of gunpowder, a critical item in any war.

[6]*The salt content of seawater is much higher near the inlets on our coast than in the bay.*

Toms River's first brush with the active side of the Revolution came in 1777, when an attack was led against the Coates Point works by Tory general Skinner. Strangely, a Tory colonel, John Morris, had a financial interest in the works and, accordingly, one John Williams marked the buildings clearly with a painted "R" and they were spared. The works rapidly resumed production for the Continental cause: such was the fine line that often existed between Patriot and Royalist.

Ships which successfully ran the gauntlet of privateers past Old Inlet, had to contend with still another batch of rebels off Cranberry. Indeed, the Island Beach coast was considered one of the most dangerous spots on the Atlantic seaboard. An appropriate British comment of 1782 well sums up the situation:

> The town...{Toms River}...consists of about a dozen houses in which none but a piratical set of banditti reside.

In the eyes of contemporary Loyalists, this could hardly have seemed too far out of line, for even the Dover militia were part-time privateers. When the *Love and Unity*, a British merchant vessel, grounded off Cranberry on August 1, 1778, the militia rowed out and floated home one of the fattest prizes ever taken in the area — eighty hogsheads of loaf sugar, seven thousand bottles of liquor; salt, flour, cheese, and much fine glassware. The loot was disposed of at an Admiralty sale in Toms River while the ship was rechristened the *Washington* and set at anchor in Barnegat Bay. The British, however, not prepared to sit by, sent two ships and two brigs to re-take the craft. William Dillon, another of our iniquitous Tory friends, who hid on the beach where Island Heights stands today, came out and guided seven armed boats through the inlet. They recaptured the prize with little difficulty, between seven and eight o'clock in the morning.

It was because of severe British reprisals that, in general, the Patriots preferred to act against Loyalist ships rather than Crown ships. At any rate, on March 1 of the next year, Isaac Potts, marshal for the sale of these prizes, put the schooner *Fanny* and the sloop *Hope* on the block, and so it went through the Revolutionary years.

To Make Ready

The Patriot element in Toms River believed that with privateering, trade, and the salt works, they could not continue to escape serious reprisals indefinitely, even if only in the form of destructive skirmishes with local Tory groups. Consequently, under the direction of Captain Joshua Huddy, a stockade was erected on a hill where Robbins Street runs today. From there it could command the river beach and a bridge, on which the shore road crossed as well. The walls stood about 7-feet high and were composed of vertical logs, sharpened on the top. There was no gate and the fort could be entered only by ladders, which were, of course, pulled in after the defenders. Within, was a low log-barrack for the tiny garrison, and a roofed cellar, which served as magazine. At the four corners were brass swivel cannons, mounted in embrasures and hurling several ounces of shot at a time. There was, to my knowledge, only one other cannon in the neighborhood, an iron gun. Other available armament consisted solely of the militia's own shoulder arms, what powder and shot could be mustered, and a few wooden pikes used to fend attackers off the walls.

Still, as the war progressed, it began to appear that the blockhouse at Toms River had been built in vain. For the most part, the privateers, meeting an adversary greater than themselves had been able to retreat in their swift whaleboats, which, with a crew of fifteen men at the oars, are said to have exceeded ten knots. They would easily lose clumsy British pursuers in the winding creeks of the saltmarsh, and few were the English sloops that would risk their bottoms in such shallows anyway.

Of course, not all escaped, and the privateer, brought to account for the error of his ways, rotted out his days aboard the ancient *New Jersey*. This former ship of the line, consigned now as a prison hulk inside Sandy Hook, became a dreaded death-trap of disease and brutality. Despite the *Jersey*, the lure of sudden wealth kept Toms River an open sore throughout the Revolution.

In November of 1781, Cornwallis surrendered to General Washington at Yorktown, and it was apparent that the war had gone to the Americans. Ben Franklin's misdirected son, William, New Jersey's last Royal Governor, had already been driven from his seat at Sweet Perth Town and was refuged in New York. It was there he made his decision to wipe out Toms River. As head of the Board of Associated Royalists he was able to muster support for this last retaliatory measure. A force was gathered in New York, composed of eighty British Regulars and forty of Dillon's Royalists, under the command of Lieutenant Blanchard of the armed whaleboats. The troops were loaded aboard the English brig *Arrogant* and managed to slip out of New York Harbor, their purpose, at least, undetected.

They hove-to off Cranberry and lowered their boats to enter the bay a little after midnight on Sunday morning, March 24, 1782. Once ashore on Coates Point, they were joined by a party of Davenport's refugees and a force of better than 120 men marched up the north shore toward sleeping Toms River.

Davenport made an attempt at effecting a surprise attack by seizing each of the sleeping houses along the way, retaining their occupants, so that no warning could be given. One man, Garret Irons, however managed to slip away and ran the whole distance to warn Captain Huddy of the impending offensive. Huddy bolted half asleep from his house and managed to rouse his pitiful garrison of twenty-five "twelve-months men."[7] They grabbed their muskets, a few powder horns that could be gathered, and made ready for battle.

[7]Men who had enlisted for twelve months and might be near the end of their term; not committed fighters.

Battle of the Blockhouse

In retrospect, we might criticize Huddy's judgment in defending the blockhouse rather than fighting Indian-style in the forest, where their unfavorable odds might not have been so heavy. As it was, they stood along the palisades as dawn came, veiled by a high web of cirrus clouds that bespoke the approach of bad weather. Blanchard's force emerged from the pines north of the blockhouse, on its exposed side; the odds, about 5-1.

The Lieutenant's call for surrender was met with Huddy's reply: "Come and take it!" Blanchard determined to do just that and opened fire. John Farr dropped from his post at the first British volley.

The Regulars managed to draw enough of Huddy's fire to exhaust his powder, and, in the exchange, killed another of his men. When the musket balls stopped coming his way, Blanchard charged the remaining colonials, who took up their pikes and traded blows amid the erratic death-rattle of musketry and slashing bayonets. John Wainwright, exposed on the palisade, fell, shot-through with six bullets; James Kinsey hung lifeless at his swivel gun, and Kennedy lay bathed in blood by a mortal wound, groaning out his last, unattended by anyone. Three more Americans fell in hand-to-hand combat before the walls were overwhelmed and the British swarmed the defenders into submission. Major John Cook was bayoneted to death after the surrender. Huddy and eleven others were taken prisoner, and five managed, miraculously, to vault the stockade and escape into the Pines.

Following the defeat, Toms River village was put to the torch. With the exception of two dwellings in the area, every building was levelled. One of those spared was the house of Aaron Buck, Dillon's brother-in-law, and the other was that of Mrs. Joshua Studson. This was reserved at the request of pirate Captain John Bacon, in token for the fact that he had killed Captain Studson in the Long Beach Massacre — a strange kindness from one who had formerly shown such brutality. The harbor was sacked, a boat being burnt on her ways, and two others carried off; one a whaleboat and the other Hyler's barge. An iron pin was driven into the vent hole of cannon and the spiked piece was tossed into the river, from which it has never been recovered.

Huddy's militia had suffered nine dead, twelve taken prisoner, and five gone free. Blanchard had lost only three men and had seven wounded. The weather was closing in, so he took no risks of making further depredations and sailed for New York that afternoon. Black Sunday at Toms River had run its bloody course.

The Sequel

After the incident at Toms River, Huddy and his men were taken back to New York and imprisoned. Governor Franklin still had not his fill of violence and ordered that Huddy hang. He was turned over to Captain John Lippincott for execution. Lippincott, in company of twenty-three Loyalists, took Huddy by boat to Sandy Hook on April 9, 1782, where he was imprisoned in the man o' war *Britannia*, which lay there at anchor.

Early on the morning of April 12, Huddy was roughly roused and put in a boat with Lippincott and a number of Loyalists. They pulled through the light mist and beached their boat at Atlantic Highlands, from where they marched Huddy to Gravelly Point. There, three fence rails were erected as a gallows and a barrel placed at the center. Huddy calmly wrote his will on its lid at Lippincott's direction. He mounted the gibbet saying: "I shall die innocent and in good cause," shook the hand of his executioner, and the noose was slipped snugly over his neck. His eye must have followed, with apprehension, the rough line running up over the sheave and down to the nervous hands that were to take his life.

A command was given, but the men hung back, hesitant to hang a man they weren't sure was dying for good reason. Lippincott cursed them and seized the line himself. Fearful hands aided him, and Huddy swung free of the barrel. Physiology predicts that briefly his blood pounded beneath the noose, striving to reach a starving brain, but the swirling world of life around him faded into nothing as he died.

Locals found him turning slowly in the afternoon sun, at about four o'clock, a note pinned to his breast swearing that the Royalists would: "hang man for man, as long as a Refugee is left existing. Up goes Huddy for Phil White." White, apparently, was the Tory justification of Huddy's execution, a man Captain Joshua had never seen, as far as can be determined. This Phil White, history records, had been shot by Colonial militiamen while trying to escape. As sometimes happens, the tale was blown out of proportion. Rumor soon had it that he had been brutally mutilated — told to run for his life after his eyes had been gouged out, then shot while helplessly stumbling away.

The hanging of Joshua Huddy ultimately brought international repercussions. Once Washington was advised of the deed, he demanded that Lippincott be handed over immediately for trial. When delays made the situation a mockery, however, it was ordered that a British prisoner of war, equal in rank to Huddy, be selected to hang in retaliation. In a colonial prison, 19-year old Captain Charles Asgill was drawn by lot as the unfortunate. "I know it would be so," he said despairingly, "I never won so much as a bet of backgammon in my life." Asgill was sent to Chatham, New Jersey, to await execution.

Charles' mother, Lady Asgill, was, of course, advised of her son's fate, and immediately petitioned King George III to order that Lippincott be given up to save her innocent son. It is said that His Majesty did this without hesitation, but that Governor Clinton failed to carry out the order.

Meanwhile, another petition was drawn up in the United States, championed by Huddy's survivors, who wanted justice, and not the senseless ending of human life. The incident became a bargaining point for the noted John Jay and Ben Franklin while they

Toms River Blockhouse

Thus it may have appeared during the summer of 1781, less than a year before its untimely demise in the early days of the following spring. On a slight rise of the river's north bank, it commands the crude pier facilities and rudimentary bridge nearby. A contemporary whaleboat is pulled against the marches and a trading ketch of some 40-feet is moored beyond, at the juncture of Jake's Branch and the main stream. The town of Toms River is not to be seen for, by our own definition, it did not exist then, being no more than a slightly increased density of population. As noted by the British account, there were only about a dozen houses in the immediate vicinity.

tried to secure an acceptable peace treaty with the Crown. Ultimately, however, the matter was placed before the King and Queen of France for arbitration, and they instructed their emissary to intercede in favor of the young man. It was largely through his efforts, coupled with growing sympathy in America, that the release of Asgill was secured on November 7, 1782. It was certainly with great relief that he returned to England a free man, no doubt with his confidence in fate restored to a large degree.

Sometime prior to the Toms River incident, the *Speedwell*, a new patriot schooner of some twenty-two tons burden, had been seized by the British. Later she was recaptured by Captain Adam Hyler of New Brunswick, who returned with her to Toms River, desirous of placing her up for sale. There was so little left of the town, however, that no lodgings could be found for those interested in the auction so, it was held in Freehold. Such was the fate of the *Speedwell,* one of the last prizes to come through Cranberry Inlet. But, by then, it didn't matter much because definitions were changing, and the privateer now stood on the brink of absolute piracy.

In the early days of March, 1783, the Revolutionary War formally ended and the shore celebrated wildly for a time. But there was understandably much bitterness left and, petitions poured into the legislature asking that former Tories and Pine Robbers be prevented from returning to their homes. By 1800, however, sounds of discord had died to an occasional bitter wail and, of necessity, our young nation, and the shore as well, turned inward to grow.

Chapter 8

The Iron Masters

Bog Ore

[1]*It is likely this color comes from humic substances leached from vegetal debris by acidic soil and bog conditions throughout the Pines.*

There is a saying, down Barnegat way, that the bay takes its rusty brown hue from "thin iron" leached out of the bogs, and there is perhaps an element of truth therein since the bogs are rich with iron in many locales.[1] Since glacial times, the numberless streams that wind through the gentle hills of our pines have brought toward the sea a continual burden of ferric sulfate, dissolved slowly from the sandy soil. Where the streams fan out sluggishly in the salt marsh, the sulfates are subjected to a reducing action set up by decaying vegetation. When the products of this reaction are exposed to air by movement of the water, they become Fe_2O_3, which rapidly precipitates out on the creek bed as a thick reddish sludge: bog ore.

Bog ore, or "limonite," as geologists term it, ranges in consistency from a near-liquid, through hard "slab," to a cement-like conglomerate of ore-bonded sand and pebbles. In the beds, and along cove banks where deposits form, it is usually laid down between two and six inches thick. Such a bed, of reasonable extent, would take between one and two hundred years to form.

This points up the unique nature of bog ore, in that it is one of our only self-replenishing natural resources, representing a completely natural concentration of very low grade material that can produce a high grade ore. (For18th- and 19th century technicians, hardrock — high-grade ores from the Piedmont — were virtually inextractable.) Minus the gross impurities, such as rock and gravel, the final "shot ore" is of extremely high quality. Man, in future generations, may well return to the bogs as his seemingly vast supplies of rock ore dwindle.

While praising the element iron, it would be a shame to ignore a further virtue of bog iron, as extolled by local legend. This is the premise that it does not rust, but forms a protective oxide on the surface, which tends to retard extensive corrosion. The metal bands on the furnace at Allaire seem, in some measure, to have borne this out. After a hundred years exposure, they possess a rather solid black coating on their surface. The most plausible explanation of this phenomenon lies in the fact that the bog iron is close to wrought iron in consistency. That is, the bog iron has a low carbon content and a small proportion of slag. It is a tough metal, highly resistant to shock, and showing some ability to withstand corrosion. American iron, mined later in our history, became more like cast iron, with a higher proportion of carbon.

Origins

The settlers recognized early the value of bog ore deposits. What was possibly the first forge was started in 1676 by Lewis Morris, a colonist under the Monmouth Patent. The early furnaces were tremendously crude affairs, frequently just a large, hollowed gum tree, lined with clay and erected on a clay hearth about one foot thick. They possessed two sets of tap holes, one near the base, through which the molten iron was drawn off, and one higher up through which the slag[2] was tapped. Draft was provided through large hand-powered bellows. The furnaces once lit, were continually fired and could be kept in blast from six to eighteen weeks at a time. In the 1600s this iron was produced in the form of a white-hot incandescent sponge, removed from the furnace and pounded at a forge to remove the impurities, leaving a breed of wrought iron. The fur-

[2]The more or less completely fused and vitrified matter separated during the reduction of a metal from the ore.

naces were tapped about every nine or ten hours while in blast.

As the industry entered the 18th century, larger brick furnaces from 20- to 24- feet square were introduced. The elimination of hand-operated bellows and the development of new heat-resistant alloys now made blasts of seven and eight months possible. In general, the length was limited only by the period when water power was available, to give the needed forced draft. The furnaces customarily went in blast about the middle of April and were usually kept so 'til nearly year's end when the streams froze over. As the fires needed continual attention, there was always a celebration when the furnaces were "blown out."

In building a furnace, a location was selected against rising ground, where possible, so that wagon loads of the charge material could be introduced directly from a ramp at the appropriate level. The basis for all furnaces was the hearth, a solid base of available native stone, from which was erected the body of brick and sand insulating materials. The throat was lined with slate, or some form of firebrick, to withstand the terrific heat of the blast. It was narrow at the bottom, where the crucible[3] was set, and a gate was installed to draw off the molten product. Just above this, the throat widened into the "bosh"[4] which ranged from six to nine feet in diameter. Near the lower end of this, bleeders for slag ran out and the tuyer, a venting duct, was placed.

[3] A hollow area at the bottom of a furnace in which the molten metal collects.

[4] The section of a blast furnace between the hearth and the stack.

The tuyer existed for the introduction of forced draft which was supplied by large bellows, tub-like in form, operated by a nearby waterwheel. The charge[5] in such a furnace was frequently about two and a half tons of ore and 180 bushels of charcoal. The end product was a ton of iron of 40 percent grade. When in blast, weighing and addition of charge went on day and night, conducted by tradesmen known as "fillers".

[5] Quantity of material.

Periodically, the gate was opened and with a roar of flame, the molten iron poured out through runners and into molds that were dug right out of the sandy floor. Someone once likened the furnace and iron to a sow and her pigs. Over the years the metaphor was corrupted, until the crude chunks produced in those sand molds were called "sows" and the smaller ones "pigs," hence the widely used term "pig iron."

Nearby was a cupola where the pigs were re-heated and reduced by pounding beneath a four- to six-hundred pound trip hammer activated by a cam on the waterwheel. When the impurities were driven out, the product became "bar iron," suitable for turning out goods. Some was sent to slitting mills, or rolling mills, where it was transformed into rod, for cutting into nails, etc.. A two thousand pound barrel of such rod sold for $105 in 1794.

Heat around such structures soon dried out timbers, making them highly susceptible to fire. The Martha Furnace diary on June 2, 1813, makes a telling point:

> Great conflagration, The Furnace and warehouse was this day entirely consumed, but fortunately no lives lost. John Craig got very much burnt.

The pressures of the economy were great however, for Martha Furnace went in blast again on August 11 of the same year.

A furnace in blast required about twenty thousand acres of pineland to support its fires, and kept the woodcutters busily employed in cutting for its demands. As early as 1700, the ore itself sold for $6.50 per ton while the finished pig went for £18. Both ore and the iron itself were customarily transported by water, explaining the favor in which stream and riverside locations were held. To move a ton twenty road miles cost some 30 shillings while, by barge,[6] the fee for the same load and distance was only 5 shillings.

[6] *One of these 19th century ore barges was found by archaeologists and preserved at Batsto, now part of a well-interpreted state park complex.*

In 1719, we find the colonial bog furnaces bitterly opposed by British ironmongers, who felt sharply the inroads on their market. Still, even in 1750, the importation of the needed "pig" was permitted, duty free, by the Crown. The cycle was most convenient for other — and more influential — merchant groups in England.

Following the traditional mercantile policy, raw materials came in from the colonies. In this case, the pig iron was shipped at extremely low rates as ballast in returning ships. On the outward voyage the ships carried goods that had been fabricated in Britain from the colonial iron, thus boosting the mother country at the expense of would-be American manufacturers. This, as already discussed, had some bearing on the Revolution.

The Iron Masters

Partly in consequence of, and, to a large extent, in spite of the international factors, bog iron establishments continued to mushroom in size and complexity. Gradually, the producer gathered about him an increasing community of workers, requiring an ever widening need for a self-sustaining social and economic structure. What resulted was virtually a feudal situation with the bog iron centers assuming quite the role of a medieval manor.

Charles Read was born in Philadelphia in 1715, the son of a merchant who had failed, following a devious life in politics. In 1766, Read started his bog empire in the pines with his Etna (Aetna) Furnace. Batsto Furnace, too, was started in that year, and, by 1768, Taunton and Atsion were all in operation. Read, it is said, provided the greatest single impetus to the bog iron industry in South Jersey, but as an individual he had financially overextended himself and spent the rest of his life in misery, dying an indebted man in North Carolina on December 27, 1774.

Batsto, in other hands, continued strongly in blast. A Philadelphia paper of the period lists nineteen separate products put out by forges in the area, including durable cast iron pipe that replaced miles of wooden ducts in Camden and Philadelphia during the Revolution. Batsto rolled out tons of cannon shot for the cause, and her skilled workers were considered of such worth that they were deferred from military service. Still, they banded together with the militia at Chestnut Neck, if only to protect their interests.

Much of the work at such forges in colonial times was performed by slaves and indentured servants. The latter signed their lives away, quite literally, for three years, to pay their passage to the New World. For their labors they received meager food and lodging, and, at the end of their labors not a cent, except in kind entitlement of a suit of clothes to replace the rags they had likely nursed the whole three years. Since they were often treated quite miserably, the desire to escape their bondage was no doubt overwhelming in many cases. When one Batsto servant ran away, a periodical offered his description and a liberal reward of $4 for his return to one William Doughty.

Following the Revolution, however, the situation was modified, and a new labor vehicle, the wage-slave, came into prominence. Bonded not by force, and far from exploited in a negative sense, he was held in the community only by economic necessity. Batsto, at her peak, employed a force of nearly 1,500 men. Skilled workers in the varied trades were paid from $20 to $25 per month, mostly in kind, for there was little trading opportunity other than in the company run stores.

In Batsto's 19th-century years she was owned by the Richards family. John Richards, nephew of Colonel William Richards (who owned Batsto and Atsion), in 1813 established Gloucester Furnace, which employed about 125 workers. In the mid-19th century, Thomas S. and Jesse Richards became co-owners and supervisors of the varied operations at Batsto. According to available records, the two lived rather well for the times and locale. They possessed some eleven female servants, and put down on the expense account outlays for eighteen gallons of French brandy at $1.75 apiece; venison, a local product, was only a dollar; ducks, $6; honey $3.27 and, in the interests of self-admiration, a looking glass $3.78. Perhaps to rectify the implications of their favored existence, they contributed "50 cents regularly per agreement" to the Methodist and Catholic churches in Pleasant Mills.

The furnace that supported this lifestyle was described following its installation on February 24, 1835. The "hearth," probably referring to the crucible itself, was 19 inches square at the bottom and 22 inches square at the top. It "beveled" to 24 inches. The "hearth," in another reference, stood 4 feet, 11 inches high "...cut 12 1/2 inches from the bottom, 9 1/2 inches from the backwall ...Boshes put in 9 inches from bevel of 2 inches in hearth, to the foot." There was a gate, of course, to retain the molten iron. The prior terminology does not seem very clear, but perhaps you get some idea what this device was like!

At Batsto a day book was kept; somewhat along the lines of a journal of events. "No. 2" of this series, which by the grace of the powers-that-be, has come down to us with a record dating from May 6, 1830. Many interesting sidelights of life at the furnace are revealed.

It was the company's policy to pay $1 to workers who went to vote on election day. Trouble was, the employee had to hire a replacement to fill in while he was gone. This cost $1.50 but, despite the added burden, one Samuel Cove, a "siller," or stoker, at the furnace, felt he needed the day off. The respite, however, did him little good - the following day, the book records Sam's replacement getting another $1.50 while Sam recovered from "the election day frolic." Other workers at Batsto took their diversion in a less strenuous manner, despite the burdens of a ten-hour day on the job. At least six of them got together and hired a singing master, each paying the same hefty fee of 87 cents for the lessons ensuing.

Batsto, by 1840, had branched out into several other fields of endeavor beyond bog iron. Excess charcoal, a corollary product left over from stoking the blast furnace, was also marketed outside, as were bricks and the issue of at least two sawmills which were generally in operation. The store books record the names of nineteen ships that were engaged running lumber and cast-iron pipe out of the Mullica.

Jesse Richards may have been a man of foresight, or he may have been already grappling with economic necessity, when, in 1846 he set up a glass factory at Batsto. Iron was ultimately destined to die out of the pines and there was no sense being caught with one's proverbial pants down. However, Jesse's efforts met with some difficulty, and, in 1847, after some fourteen fires on the premises, he was faced with a strike by the blowers. We are not told what the specific issues were, but apparently all were satisfactorily resolved for, according to records, Batsto produced 100,000 square feet of window pane per month in 1848. Experts consider the output quite phenomenal for the period and methods in use.

Nevertheless, as far as Jesse was concerned, Marx[7] had a point, and Batsto went into receivership in 1868. On February 23, 1874, a fire broke out in the village and by dawn, seventeen houses were reduced to ashes. A few buildings survived and, in 1876, the gristmill, barns, store, one house and Jesse's old mansion became part of the vast Wharton Tract. The furnace had blown out for the last time in 1858 and the stack had long crumbled to rubble. Batsto and her empire were dead.

[7]*Karl Marx: German philosopher who said "the seeds of its own collapse are inherent in a capitalist enterprise."*

At Martha

Around 1760, ten miles up Wading River, there arose the structure of Belangee's Sawmill. Around 1790, the location was purchased by Isaac Potts, a Philadelphia iron merchant, who had operated, in company with others, another sawmill at Valley Forge from 1768 until after the Revolution. Isaac erected a suitably attended furnace along a creek off Wading River and named it, as was often the custom, after his wife Martha. How proud Mrs.

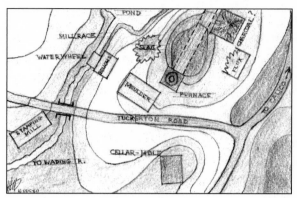

*Plan of Martha
Furnace and
surroundings.*

Potts must have been when her fat little furnace went in blast about ten o'clock on the morning of September 29,1793.

The furnace employed about sixty hands and had usually two "founders" who worked alternate twelve-hour shifts. As our little map above shows, a road wound off through the Pines to "Calico," a residential area that comprised the worker's settlement. Most of the employed were Irish, but there was also a small group of blacks. Only on rare occasion were any of the workers privileged by the attendance of a doctor.

In the summer of 1795, Potts expanded his plant with the addition of the Wading River Forge and Slitting Mill, an establishment often overlooked by historians. The forge had four fires in operation and the slitting mill was possessed of a nail-cutting machine by 1797. Earlier, nails were cut by hand and the heads pounded to shape with a hammer. Ezekiel Reed, in 1786, modernized the operation by mechanizing it. Needless to say, the forge and mill were good customers for Martha's iron until they went out of business around 1832.

Isaac Potts' land holdings were considerable, ranging from 20,000 acres in 1796, to a peak of 60,000 acres. Continued expansion of the plant was contemplated at the lake where a lock was to be built "to admit boats of ten tons burden to pass from the Furnace to the tide, (thus affording)...easy and cheap transportation."

It is presently disputed that the lock was ever built, although there is, at least, a record that one Godfrey Estlow built locks to scow ore to Martha Furnace. At any rate, it is certain that old Tuckerton road, which the establishment fronted, received much wagon traffic as the products were hauled, mostly to Wading River landing, a distance of about three miles. Records show this traffic continuing after 1808, so, if the locks were ever dug, it is quite possible they were not long in use.

Martha Furnace diary covers the period 1808 through 1815,

after the entirety had been deeded by Potts to four other men in November, 1800, who had in turn sold the unsuccessful venture in 1805. At that moment, the holdings had dropped to 15,000 acres. The records were kept by Caleb Earle, who acted as clerk during that period, and we gain much insight from his frank, if crude, prose. It is only by fortune that either the Martha Diary or the Batsto Day Book are preserved, for they were salvaged from an old safe in the Harrisville paper mills just a brief time before those buildings were gutted by fire in 1910.

Appropriately, Martha turned out hundreds of cast iron pots from her molding house and many a stout and durable stove. On December 10, 1808, Earle writes: "Cramer & Lukers team hauling cannon wheels." Thus, the implication of a more bellicose product.

Amusement was hard to come by for the hearty folks at Calico and, indeed, there was little to do in South Jersey other than drink and ... well, the reader will pardon if I quote Caleb directly on April 12, the spring of 1813:

...Wm. Mick's widow arrived here in pursuit of J. Mick who she says has knocked her up.

This wasn't new either: Let's flash back a few pages:

May 18, 1808: report says James McGilligan made a violent attempt on the chastity of Miss Durky Trusty, ye African.

May 25, 1812: James McEntire brought his daughter home from the Half Moon for fear her morals would be corrupted.

January 13, 1813: McEntire himself was sick after his election day frolic.

By July 13, he was "staggering drunk" and in 1815, it was still "McEntire drunk."

Poor Jim might have set a better example himself but at any rate the one he apparently set forth went not unheeded for on July 27, 1811, we read:

William Rose and his father both drunk and lying on the crossway. The old woman at home drunk.

Perhaps thus did our friends escape the economic unrest about them. In the interim, Martha had changed hands in 1808 and did so again in 1829. With the dawn of the 1840s, Martha sputtered

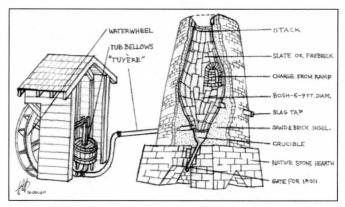

Schematic of the bog iron furnace and its major components. (After Pierce and Allaire Furnaces)

out her last monogrammed pig and gave up the ghost. Her charcoalers hung on until 1848, producing for the Philadelphia market. A final sale broke up the remaining acreage into thirty-four separate tracts, some of which are privately held to this day.

And Among the Sheltering Pines

Such were two of the larger establishments, but the Pines were honeycombed with others, quite literally one every couple of miles. Some were only forges, performing operations on "pig" produced by nearby furnaces, while others had both facilities. The ownership of many betrayed sometimes complex interlocking relations, the exact nature of which is often obscure, but all served the purpose of tapping the labor market and boosting a nascent economy. Many of those existing during the "bog iron age" are scheduled below with a paragraph or two of sidelights inserted where I have run across something of interest.

Some classic Pine Barrens facilities and dates of operation

Name	Operators	Dates of operation
Atsion	Charles Read	1765-1846
Bamber (Ferrago)	John Lacey	1810-1865
Batsto	Charles Read	1766-2858
Bergen (Washington)	Jesse Richards	1814-?(rebuilt 1832)
	William Irwin	
	Joseph Brick	1832-1854

As can be seen, Bergen dates back a bit under her first owner. Between 1814 and 1825 she was engaged in making cast iron pipe, which was sold to the city of New

York for water mains. Some of it is still in use. In those days, the produce was hauled over a corduroy road to the nearby Metedeconk River and boated to market. When Brick purchased Washington Furnace, he renamed it Bergen Iron Works, purportedly after the reputation in which Bergen iron of a different origin was held.

| Birmingham (Retreat) | Bolton and Jones | 1800-1832 |
| Butcher's | John Lippincott | 1808-1840s |

When Butcher's first went in business, she sailed her "pig" out of Cranberry Inlet, but in 1812, when the passage closed, was forced to sail all the way to Barnegat and then north again to reach New York. This was a distance of 42-miles to reach a point at the sea, just opposite the Metedeconk's mouth, and only about 5 miles east of the forge.

Butcher's was located at Butcher and Burr's Damsite, which had created a mill pond three miles long, making it the largest in New Jersey. On its surface, wood was boated from the Pines to feed the forge, located on the Metedeconk's south bank, just east of the old 'Squan-Toms River road. The dam itself was provided with a gristmill, two nearby stores, and twenty other dwellings. Charcoaling, cedar logging, shipbuilding, and even salt-harvesting helped to keep the populace busy.

Budd's Iron Works	Eli Budd	1785-1840
Bordentown	Potts, Coxe, Allen	1725-1748-50
Cohansie	(unknown)	1773-before 1789
Dover Forge	William L Smith	1809-1868
Drinker's	Edward Drinker	1780s - ?

Dover Forge was on Cedar Creek, established by Gen. John Lacey and his son-in-law, William L. Smith. Bog ore came from Double Trouble Swamp, wagons brought oyster and clam shell flux and the furnaces fired with local charcoal.

Drinker's was in the Mullica basin, along with Martha and Batsto. Drinker cast parts for John Fitch's early steamboat, which blundered about crudely on the Delaware at some seven miles per hour. He built the boat in 1786 and it operated at least until 1790.

Aetna (Tuckahoe)	Coates, Howell	1816-1832
Aetna (Medford Lakes)	Charles Read	1766-7-1773
Federal Forge	David Wright	1789 - ?
Federal Furnace	Ivins, Godfrey	1795 - before 1855
Gloucester	John Richards	1813-1848
Hampton	(unknown)	prior 1795/ 1828
Hanover	Ridgeway, Howell, Lacey, Earl	1791-2, 1863
Lisbon	John Earl	1800-before 1831
Martha	Isaac Potts	1793-1840s

Mary Ann	Benjamin Jones	1827- 1860s
Mount Holly	Pearson, Stacy, Burr	1730-1778

Mount Holly suffered a violent end for, in 1778, the British destroyed it completely and it was never re-established.

[8]*Before 1811*
[9]*In ruins by 1855*

New Mills (Pemberton)	John Lacey	1781/1787[8]
Phoenix	(unknown)	1816-1817[9]
Speedwell	Ben Randolph	1785- 1839
West Creek (Stafford)	John Lippincott	1797-1838

Stafford Forge cranberry bogs today cover whatever might remain of old Stafford Forge, which lay some seven miles south of the town of Barnegat. Mr. Lippincott did a land office business while he remained, but that was only for the short span of ten years.

Taunton	Charles Read	1766/1767
Union	William Cook, Sr.	1800 - ?
Wading River Forge	Isaac Potts	1795-1825/30
Weymouth — Shoemaker, Robeson, Ashbridge, Paul		1800-62

Weymouth is an appropriate one with which to finish this capsule survey, for she was the last furnace in the Pines to go out, dying in the year 1865. The twenty-nine establishments discussed above probably comprise a nowhere- near complete record of those that actually operated, but they give the reader an idea of the scope of the industry. None, of course, rivaled U.S. Steel in production but they formed a significant segment of the coastal and national economy during their life span.

Tale of Another Bog Iron Empire

Stretching the scope of this book slightly, we poke our nose up the headwaters of the Manasquan River, to an area known, since before 1650, by the Lenape name of *Squankum*. Here, along the bank of a winding creek, one Isaac Palmer built a sawmill in 1750. Around 1800, a stack was erected near the site, taking the name of Monmouth Furnace. A few years later, iron components for a steam engine were cast for one John Stevens, who incorporated them in his early steamship, the *Phoenix*.

Unfortunately, Stevens was unable to operate the *Phoenix* on the Hudson River, as he had intended, since a monopoly on steamship traffic in these waters had been obtained by a competitor, Chancellor Livingston. Consequently, in 1809, Stevens sent the

Phoenix to sea with his son, Robert, in command. Once outside Sandy Hook, she became the world's first ocean-going steam vessel. It was Stevens' intent to head south and operate her in the Delaware, but a northeaster offshore forced her to take shelter inside treacherous Barnegat Inlet, thus making her, incidentally, the first steamer to enter the bay. When the storm had passed, she again put to sea and completed her voyage without further misadventure.

Meanwhile, James P. Allaire, the descendent of a French Huguenot family which had emigrated to America late in the 1600s, entered the brass foundry of one Robert Fulton as a helper. With his own hands, he cast the cylinder of Fulton's historic *Clermont* in the year 1807. Fulton became a close friend of Allaire and, when he died in 1815, he made the latter executor of his estate and heir to the foundry. Subsequently, Allaire changed the name of these works to James P. Allaire Works, moving the facilities to Corlears Hook on New York's East River.

Apparently, Fulton had some connections with the Monmouth Furnace, since he had spent his honeymoon there, in a tiny foreman's cottage which may be seen to this day. At any rate, in 1821 the works were leased to Benjamin Howell, who re-named them "Howell Works." Allaire, in the interests of supplying iron for his growing industrial complex, purchased them the following year, retaining, for a time the name intact. Allaire's New York foundry was fast becoming the world's leading producer of marine engines and boilers. By 1818, it had already served the famed Savannah, the first steam-auxiliary to cross the Atlantic.

At the time Allaire purchased them, the original Howell Works probably consisted of fourteen or fifteen frame buildings. By 1831, Howell Works post office had been established, alleviating the need for a post rider who, until then, made the circuit between Freehold and Toms River. During the period 1834-1837, the growing village at what became known as Allaire had reached a peak. There were about fifty dwellings, and the works supported a force of some five hundred men, citizens of what was then termed a perfect example of the bog iron community.

During Allaire's heyday, banks were hard to get to, and often unreliable. Accordingly the village printed its own money, or more accurately, "orders for services" which were neatly engraved with a picture of the furnace, and signed by "James P." personally. They ranged in denomination from 6 1/2 cents to $10 and were valid for goods purchased in the company store; a large, well inventoried building of four stories.

Allaire had a fair sized church, which bore the name Christ Episcopal Church, and a small but effective pipe organ within which had been built by Henry Erben, a gentleman who had attained some note in that profession. The bell in the steeple had been cast in the town's foundry, alloying gold with bog iron to produce the desired tone. Strangely, with the passage of time, the solid iron clapper rusted away to nothing. The preacher was retained on an annual salary of $500. He doubled this by serving as schoolmaster to a class that numbered up to a hundred pupils.

The Allaire works were once valued at $250,000, and supported a large number of tradesmen whose crafts are somewhat esoteric today: ore-raisers, colliers, molders, fillers, and ware cleaners. Apprentices to the furnace workers paid an initiation fee of $60 in order to have the opportunity to enter one of the trades.

The furnace itself rose some fifty feet on a massive base of stone block. It stood against steeply rising ground, which permitted easy introduction of locally burned charcoal from a depot nearby. The stack and molding area were housed in a large four-story structure. The effluent from a two-stage lake, or reservoir, powered great bellows that sustained a roaring draft through the fires.

A smithy shop was located a few hundred yards from the casting house, attending to the equestrian needs of the community and housing the Allaire Fire Company. Some years ago, before the state took an active interest in the then abandoned town, I entered this old structure, part of which was in the process of collapse from sheer decay. Amongst the scattered remains of harness fittings and horseshoes were two ancient fire wagons, emblazoned with the faded legend "Allaire Fire Co." One was, from all appearances, a hose cart, while the other, as I remember, was a hand-pumper. Since then, the old wagons have disappeared, I hope to some safe location, and the building has virtually vanished.

[10] An early hand iron, heated in a fire and used to press clothing.

Allaire's products covered a rather wide range of expression including a large proportion of "hollow ware," which included pots, kettles, and cauldrons, enamelware fired in a special furnace, and iron pipe. Screws, bolts, stoves, and "sadirons"[10] were also turned out in quantity. Much of the pig iron that was cast went to Allaire's own New York foundry.

For transporting his goods to this facility, Allaire maintained three steamships: the *Isis*, *Oris*, and *Osiris*, which ran from Long Branch to New York. The vessels made regular passages by way of the now-closed Shrewsbury Inlet, which, with a running tide, provided endless thrills to passengers aboard. Navigation through these tricky waters was facilitated in that the craft were twin-engined, allowing independent control of each paddlewheel.

Meanwhile, back at the village, Allaire[11] was ensconced with the typical opulence of an iron master. The old mansion was a rambling structure on high ground behind the furnace, a tree-lined drive sweeping rather majestically before its eminence. James Allaire no doubt went to sleep many nights with the contented roar of the fires echoing in the distance. He led a life not unlike a member of the landed aristocracy. He could ill-afford to let isolation rob him of social diversion and, on occasion, as many as fifty carriages lined the drive. Even winter brought no cessation to the plantation-like existence, the carriages being replaced with sleighs.

[11] *The 19th century bog-r-iron producing community is now a restored village in Allaire State Park.*

A Crumbling End

The bog iron industry attained its peak in the years following the war of 1812. Surprisingly, the discovery of rich rock ores in the Pennsylvania fields did not spell the end of the coastal furnaces. Perhaps the primary reason for this was the relative economy of water transport compared to rail, which was then only a primitive novelty. Some of New Jersey's own furnaces brought ore by schooner from mountains bordering the upper Hudson River.

Shortly after 1817, a British innovation introduced the "puddling" of molten iron in the center of the furnace to purify it, a process which enabled for the first time, the use of anthracite coal. Previously, burning anthracite had rendered the iron full of impurities. Allaire himself had been an early experimenter with anthracite, the material which, in competition with native charcoal, ultimately spelled the death of an industry. Basically, the coastal furnaces, if they were to effect a shift to hard coal, were faced with a "weight-losing material;" that is, they transported it all the way from distant fields just to burn it. Consequently, after 1840, a definite shift westward was apparent, and ultimately irrevocable.

There was naturally a lag of sorts, while the local furnaces rode on a subsiding wave of past reputation and an economic cushion of inexpensive water transport. Although the bog iron was actually more expensive to produce, its malleable consistency and suitability for small forges, found it catering more effectively to agricultural and home markets, thus enabling a few of the stronger empires to survive past mid-century.

An aging James Allaire watched his furnace blown out for the last time in 1848, then lived ten years more before leaving his son, Hal, to rule the empty village and seven thousand acres of land. "Prince Hal," as he became known, was an architect by profession who lived almost as a recluse in the old mansion, with a lonely old French servant to attend his needs. The once great works were frequented by only an occasional picnicker and an enterprising Frenchman who opened a small restaurant in the old wheelwright's shop.

Just before his death in 1901, Hal sold Allaire to a Mr. W.J. Harrison of Lakewood, who in turn relinquished, for consideration, the village and five-thousand acres to the noted journalist Arthur Brisbane in 1907. Brisbane leased the village and a two-hundred acre tract to the Boy Scouts in 1928 and their activities managed to stave off total decay for a few years.

Still, great deterioration had already taken place. In 1891, much of the casting house still remained, but by 1950 there was not a single beam standing, and the towering furnace stood swallowed by a marshy jungle, a hearty tree crabbed into the crumbling brickwork where it had already thrived for some years. Most of the original worker's dwellings had vanished, and only a few segments of these rather extensive multiple structures remain in the area.

At Batsto, only the gristmill, a carriage house, smith shop, the mansion and a few outbuildings survived the conflagration of 1874 and remain for the curious. Both at Batsto and at Allaire however, the state began programs of restoration in the 1950s that promise to preserve a sound image of New Jersey's old bog iron empires.

The marshy ground around Allaire's furnace has been cleared and drained, allowing the outlines of the foundation and casting floor[12] to emerge. The buildings are brightly painted and crammed with an ever-increasing store of relics. There is the inevitable gift

[12]Place where the molds for the molten iron were dug.

shop, which, of course, gives nothing for free, and there was even a wedding at the old Episcopal Church in 1960. The first such event there since February 19, 1901, when Miss Carrie Estella Stakey, of Allaire, and Mr. Charles Craig, of Lower Squankum, were united.

But these can only be symbols of what once was. At Martha, and a score of other abandoned places, nothing remains but the moldering cellar hole, an occasional slag heap, the rare and rusted cannon ball, a dried pond and sluiceway with crooked vegetation groveling about their bottoms or, perhaps, a rotten, sagging hovel that was once the abode of an iron master.

Allaire's massive furnace in 1958 (clockwise from left); Christ Episcopal Church; the foreman's cottage, on a knoll above the millpond, where Robert Fulton and his bride spent their honeymoon; Allaire's company store — the small building in the background was a bakery in 1853.

Chapter 9

From the Land

The Pine Woods

When the wealthy iron masters had passed from the Pines, they left an understandable vacuum in the local labor market. However, responsive to a new outside demand, the pinewood lot operators moved in to replace them, exploiting what was otherwise a forest of limited usefulness.

Strangely, the Pines had been responsible for most of the region's early settlement. The sawmills they drew had provided what was virtually the only available nucleus for the condensation of population away from the sea, giving not only employment but also an article of trade and fabrication. Their greatest contribution in this vein appears to have been made between 1735 and 1750. However, mills resurged in importance as cutting for the furnaces dropped off.

Ebenezer Applegate was an early bird on record, establishing his mill on Kettle Creek in 1740. A competitor, Mr. Edward was going full steam nearby in 1742. On the Metedeconk, Tunis Denise had a sawmill and gristmill, possibly at what later became Butcher and Burr's Damsite (see previous chapter). It was operating by 1755.

South of these, on the branches of Toms River, we find several more. There was Matthew Van Horne's sawmill on the Davenport Branch in 1749, Van Hook's at Dry Cedar swamp; Everingham's on the North Branch in 1750; and two others on the Ridgeway Branch in 1751.

Where the pines grew close together and escaped the ravages of fire for sufficient periods, they were forced, by their own proximity, to reach high and straight before sending out branches to the sunlight. Such long, clear-grained wood was early sought for spars and mast stock by shipbuilders. Barnegat ships from Revolutionary days traded cedar rails, salt, and pine boards to New York. In Colonial times, pinewood for fuel brought four shillings per cord of "market-wood;" later the price crept to twenty shillings, for wood delivered at the pier.

A New Demand

With the opening of new timber reserves in other sections of the country, trade from the Pines dropped off considerably and a new source of demand became necessary if the industry was to remain productive. The bog forges seemed to fill the gap for a time and, in such a primitive economy, I doubt that there was any serious dislocation.

In 1811 or 1812, the Evans high-pressure steam engine was introduced to America. Waterpower, however, continued rightfully as the dominant source of energy for many years and, even in 1840 steam power in the mid-Atlantic states cost manufacturers five to six times as much hydraulic energy. The damsite was still predominant in 1860, but by then its days were clearly numbered.

Despite the usefulness of coal as a source of heat in steam production, it was as much a weight-losing material to the manufacturer and steamship owner, as to the iron master. This, coupled with the lack of any efficient overland transport method, pointed to coastal forests and local schooners for fuel and economical transport. Simultaneous with the consequential demand for cordwood was a rapid development in sawmills. As time passed further into the 19th century, this trade in wood became available to compensate for the downslide in bog iron.

Cordwood was cut by locals at 50 cents per cord labor charge, and was shipped by the woodlot owners aboard large fleets of coasting schooners that operated in great profusion from such ports as the Mullica. The Reverend Clarence Woodmansee, a near legendary gentleman of the bay area, remembered that down on Double Creek (bordering Barnegat Bay behind Long Beach Island), there were scores of docks along the marshes, piled high with stacks of cordwood in 8-foot lengths, which ran along the trail back towards the Pines. He recalled lines of teams a half mile long winding out of the woods at sundown. At Toms River, too, sources report that teams came down to load the schooners, which bore wood in twenty-five cord lots to outside markets.

As recorded, most cordwood found its way to the fire boxes of steam engines, primarily those at sea used in propulsion and, aboard the more refined sailing ships, as donkey engines.[1] As rail transport came into its own, the use of more compact, energy-rich and efficient anthracite grew increasingly practical. Consequently, the market for cordwood began to dwindle by the 1840s.

[1] A small steam engine used for hoisting sails, cargo or anchor.

Charcoaling

It was somewhat paradoxical that the steam engine industry had once again turned to the Pines to procure a charcoal that could aid in the burning of the less-combustible coal. Charcoal was a light fuel that burned steadily, with considerable heat, where draft was applied. The demand of charcoal meant that pineland, which had dropped to ten cents an acre, went up to $6 and then as high as $25 per acre in good areas.

The art of charcoaling required first the erection of a "fergen," or central core, that was essentially a rigid pole, 6- or 7-feet high, set vertically in the ground. The kiln was built around this, consisting of closely stacked pinewood, and covered with sod "floats," set with the grass facing inward. A notched log was laid against the side so the tender could get to the apex for inspection and ignition. Since there was a virtual absence of air, the kiln burned slowly downward for several days, with new fuel being constantly introduced at the neck. Ordinarily the tender spent his time in a little lean-to beside the kiln, so he could watch for too rapid burning or

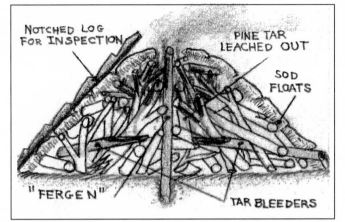

A schematic of the charcoal and tar kiln.

spreading of fire to the nearby woods. When the fire burned out, the kiln was allowed to cool carefully for a day or so. If the fresh coal were exposed while it was still hot it would crack into tiny bits, or perhaps burst into flame and negate a week's work. After cooling, all that had to be done was rake off the sand, that being all that remained of the sod, and bag or load the finished charcoal.

When charcoal was a flourishing industry, the schooners came in to landings at Waretown, Forked River, Barnegat and Toms River. The wagons that brought goods out of the Pines held the equivalent of three cords, equal to about a hundred bushels at ten cents a bushel; or $9 a wagonload. The bottoms were set sliding, with old horseshoes nailed on as handles so the load could be jettisoned by a single swift yank. The coal wagons were drawn to the docks by teams of four ill-tempered mules. Most thought them unmanageable, but the teamsters handled them without reins, employing a sharp tongue and, perhaps more significantly, a long blacksnake whip!

Tar Kilns

Often corollary to the production of charcoal was the process of extracting pine-tar, a substance sought for naval stores, and used in the manufacture of printer's ink and in lamp-black, employed in certain home remedies. In one of the latter, chicken feathers and tar were warmed in the pan of a shovel. The vapors inhaled were designed to produce some medicinal effect — nausea seems most probable — but, at any rate, results were "guaranteed."

The tar kiln was set up much the same as one for charcoal, except that a hollow log was inserted at the bottom to tap off the melted tar. This was steeped slowly from the logs, as they burned from the top down, the tar running through the unburned wood and finding its way to the drain. The kiln, tended carefully by an appointed Piney, would often burn eight or ten days before expiring.

More Recently

Today, New Jersey's 1,300,000 acres of pineland, which cover the greater part of the state's southern sector, are yielding only about ten percent of their potential, were they properly managed. Pinewood is still cut from the Pine Barrens and it is still stacked in great piles hundreds of yards long and 7- or 8-feet high, now awaiting heavy flatbed trucks rather than the more colorful lumber schooner.[2]

[2]*Pine cordwood stacks were still seen in Brick Township when* Closed Sea *was written, but today this land is all beneath shopping malls.*

Much cordwood goes into the pulpwood market providing an annual income to the state of $400,000. Firewood comprises an equal amount, and Christmas trees, where the pines are in proper variety and form, a total of $700,000. Charcoal at this late date produces a revenue of $100,000 annually. Both charcoal and firewood, once thought to be rather dead fields, are enjoying a recent revival with the meteoric boom in home fireplaces and barbecues. Charcoal seems to have a special appeal with the flavor it is said to impart. Its manufacture also conserves natural resources, since even branches and twigs make efficient fuel, especially when reprocessed into briquettes.

The Cedar Swamps

Barnegat's ancient cedar swamps thrived in low areas, which, in eons past, locals believed had been arms to the sea. A rising land had, they said, drained these channels leaving moist valleys and mud-choked streams. The cedars abounded under such conditions and soon dotted the dank depressions. It was said that over the centuries, parent trees were in competition with their offspring, all climbing upward to the light, and the cedar swamp was born. It

A section of the Manahawkin cedar swamp in 1958, freshly cut back and exposing the long, straight timber to view. It is now part of the Edwin B. Forsythe National Wildlife Refuge.

is more likely, however, that in post-glacial New Jersey, rising sea level inundated low areas, making valleys increasingly wet and stimulating the accumulation of deeper and deeper layers of silt and peat beneath the forests.

In the 19th century there were many of these areas, varying from half an acre to six miles in extent. The trees grew closely spaced in a nearly aquatic situation: dark, brandy-colored water with a bottom of soft black ooze, choked with fallen trees and gnarled roots. All was coated with an eternal green algae, even to the surface of the quiet water. A boat could pass with ease but the green mantle closed behind, leaving not a trace of its passage. Tangled laurel rose sometimes fifteen or twenty feet, making travel through some areas all but impossible. The patriarch cedars themselves rose fifty or sixty feet without a branch, then spread out into a great matted crown which admitted only a chosen few shafts of light. When the southerlies blew, the whole forest groaned and sighed in a weird melancholy. On calm days, silence hovered with an aura of death. Some of the trees were monstrous, the ages of a select few exceeding a thousand years. Perhaps the most famous of the area's swamps is the 'Hawkin swamp, which lies between Manahawkin and Barnegat Bay. It has been cut over for some two hundred years and still retains a vast measure of its primeval spell. Where limited areas have been stripped, they have often become an impenetrable wall of holly and swamp huckleberry.

The cedar swamps were early recognized as a valuable resource. In 1791, some seventeen ships regularly carried timber to New

[3]The Silent Maid, circa 1924, has been maintained by David Beaton's shipwright grandson, Tommy, and sailed into the new millennium with most of her original planks, at this juncture over three quarters of a century old.

York from the Egg Harbor cedar swamps near the Mullica. For well in excess of a century, the local swamp cedar planked local ships. My father's great catboat, the *Silent Maid*, has borne her swamp-cedar strakes for thirty years in health.[3]

Recently, Dave Beaton, a Scotsman of near-legendary renown in the yacht racing world, informs me that you can't get local cedar for boat building. Perhaps just as well, given the few stands left of any account. Dave speaks with some authority and, since he finds cedar a bit tricky to work with despite its durability, the remnant may well stay intact until swallowed by housing developments.

Cedar Mining

Even before 1800, the better stands of cedar were waning, and locals in search of larger trees were forced into the actual mining of virtually prehistoric specimens that had lain submerged beneath the muck for many centuries. The baymen, in fact, maintained that these trees were remnants of the great flood survived by Noah in biblical times.

Cedar mining, in Ocean and southern Burlington counties, became a real industry in the last quarter of the 19th century. One wonders how the excavation of a single log in such moist, unsure earth was economical, but time was cheap in those days and the logs were often immense. In 1885, our state geologist found, near Dennisville, a log 1,080-years old. A local in the same area uncovered another, 6 feet in diameter, with 1,100 annual growth rings. The stature of such a leviathan must have been fantastic!

The "miner" located his target by means of a long iron probe, which usage colloquialized to "progue." With this device, he determined the direction and extent of the trunk. Next, a long saw, such as was used for cutting ice from winter ponds, was passed into the soil and the top and roots were removed. Now a ditch was dug, exposing the entire log and, shortly thereafter, seepage from the marshy soil had filled the depression.

Two facts present themselves at this point: First, a cedar log that had been completely buried was always preserved enough to float when pried loose. Second, the logs, when free, would always roll 180°, coming to rest at the water's surface bottom-side up. Since

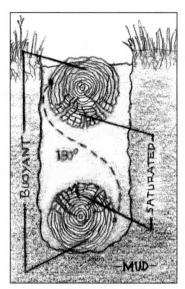

A diagram showing how the ancient cedar logs turned through 180° when freed from their resting places.

no one seems to offer an explanation of the latter phenomenon, I may as well attempt it.

When the tree first fell — whether it was a "windfall," with roots torn loose, or a "breakdown," with trunk actually severed from the anchorage — one side was obviously imbedded in mud or water, protecting it from the combined debilitating effects of air and rain. It seems conceivable that the upper, exposed side may have been at least partially saturated before the entire was buried. Thus, when the log was freed, with no branches to obstruct its turning, the more heavily saturated upper side would gravitate downward yielding a revolution through 180°.

At any rate, the fellows had a log now, which somehow they had to transport to more workable territory. Chroniclers are not specific on the point, but it would seem that pries and many rope slings may have served to remove the leviathans from their watery graves. Next, the leached and decayed wood was peeled off in useless slabs from the core of pungent wood. Then the sound core was cut into movable lengths and dragged somewhat laboriously from the swamps.

Most mined cedar went to splitters for making into shingles, which sold for between $13 and $15 a thousand. A good man could just about produce that many in a week, and a good log would last him quite a while. Some maintained that such shingles would last a full century, but, even the baymen vouched for no more than sixty or sixty-five years — still a fair lifetime for a thin, unpainted bit of wood that had already spent perhaps a thousand years underwater. Eventually, the intrusion of machine shingle-splitters and the opening of northern lumber reserves spelled the end of this unique endeavor.

Moss Gatherers

During the summer months, *Sphagnum papillosum* grows in the cedar swamps, and in years past it was gathered by farmers living nearby using 3- to 5-tined potato rakes. They piled it loosely on small sunny hillocks to dry, after which it was baled in thirty or thirty-five pound bales. In 1945, these sold for between sixty and seventy cents each. Domestically, sphagnum moss has been long used as a dressing for boils and weeping wounds. It has great absorptive power, capable of taking up to twenty-two times its own weight in water, more than three times the capacity of an equal amount of cotton. It was used extensively during World War I as a filler for surgical dressings, and more recently as a grafting and rooting aid to nurserymen. Despite its apparent advantages over cotton, it is not employed today in dressings.[4]

[4]*Sphagnum today is still a nurseryman's staple, much coming from outside this region.*

Salt Haying

You will perhaps remember the testimony of John Barclay and Arthur Forbes, back in Chapter 2:

> ...Barnagat or Burning-Hole, is said to be a very good place for fishing; and there (sic) is some desiring to take up land there, who inform that it is good land, (sic) and abundance of meadow lying to it...(March 29, 1684).

An "abundance of meadow," indeed! Even in 1870, there were some 44,515 acres in Ocean County and Egg Harbor alone. Spreading for miles in a broad green carpet, this fine wiry salt hay springs up wherever a sedge of decomposed vegetable matter has been deposited above the bay's water level. The result is an abundant crop requiring no maintenance, which is virtually impervious to nature's ravages and which, through its inherent mineral content, eliminates the need for "salting" of livestock that have grazed thereon. *Spartina patens* thrives most under the propitious conditions of a dry summer, oddly enough, and following regeneration provides and holds its own humus by means of last year's blades. It is highly resistant to killing frosts, which so often raise havoc with man-initiated crops.

The Dutch and Swedes, earlier European visitors to our shore, took salt hay by boat on the Mullica and Wading Rivers. "We met this Jacob Hendricks in a canoe with hay," said Mr. Jasper Daukaerts in 1679. Increased capacity was of course obtained when large scows came on the scene.

Into the early years of the 19th century, the grass was mowed with hand-slung scythes, piled on poles in little stacks and carried to the boats, which remained the only practical way to get the hay to market (even the broadest tired wagons required a laboriously constructed road into the marsh) Author Harold Wilson measured a 19th century scow which he found to be 33-feet long, 12-foot in beam, and 3-feet between decks. Unseamanlike as it may seem to the initiate, the scows were apparently caulked from the inside, since facilities were not available to haul them for a proper job. No doubt, some of the caulking worked loose in time, but at least it stopped the influx for a while. There were two access hatches in the deck for the purpose of entrance for caulking. "And a hell of a job that was!" one local recalls, thinking no doubt of a summer sun beating down on the deck above that narrow pit, with filthy slop around his ankles and the stench of rotten hay and mold in his nostrils! The deck and topsides of the scows were planked in 2-inch cedar, while the bottom was of Jersey pitch pine, to resist marine borers in the absence of anti-fouling paints. In shallow water, the barges were poled with 15-foot cedar pikes and, after the introduction of cheap engines, towed by a garvey. A few were rigged for sailing of sorts.

As the 19th century advanced, less ambitious locals introduced the horse and ox-drawn mowing machines. Hand and horse-pow-ered balers were also introduced, which greatly simplified the han-dling of a bulky cargo. The teams for mowing wore no shoes, but when the marshes were soft, they had flat "mud boots" fastened to their hind feet, which acted like snowshoes and kept them on top of the marshy ground. Teams proved best for haying even with the coming of tractors for the latter were quite liable to sink ignomini-ously in a pothole.

The market for salt hay was quite extensive. In the early years, of course, it was primarily fodder but later it was used by certain souls who made iron pipe by the "pitcast" method. As commercial packing, it has been used for glassware, pottery, and even bananas. It also has found extensive employment in road construction and was shipped to the coastal resorts, where it was spread on the dunes to prevent shifting once man had removed the natural cover. Coastal fishermen even packed it around their wooden-slabbed ice houses, helping their supply last well into the warmer months.

Harrisville Story

Perhaps the strangest employment of salt hay was made in the Mullica basin, at places like Pleasant Mills, and Harrisville on the Wading River. Here it was processed into oddly-shaded brown wrapping paper. At one time the Pleasant Mills Works were owned by a Philadelphia daily newspaper, and their journal was printed on the product of New Jersey's marshes. All together, the mills were served weekly by more than forty loaded scows of hay.

Harrisville had its beginnings in 1832, with a stock capitalization of $65,000, and was one of the earliest machine paper mills erected. William McCarty was the founder and, accordingly, the village was named McCartyville. By 1835, capitalization was up to $95,000 and a huge double-paper mill 240-feet long turned out nearly a ton of paper daily.

The establishment also had a gas plant, which produced for lighting purposes. How strange the glowing mantles among desolate pines! A carpenter shop, grist mill, stone warehouse, boarding house, dwellings for the superintendent and workers, and a store that rolled in $3000 a year in profits completed the picture. Later in 1835, the corporation was reorganized with a capitalization of $200,000; $25,000 of which was offered to the public in 1837. The corporation was the "Wading River Manufacturing and Canal Corporation." The canal bit referred to a U-shaped excavation about 20-feet wide, which funneled the waters of the Wading River to huge turbines underneath the mill, providing power for two 10-foot mixing vats.

The heavy-grade paper was similar to butcher's wrapping paper and was formed, in various varying degrees of stiffness, as binder board[5] and ladies' bonnet boards. Some writing paper was produced, but all had an odd yellowish cast caused by the iron-tainted

[5] *A stiff form of cardboard used in book binding.*

cedar-water. It was hoped the company could expand into silk, but further extensions got them into trouble. It was at this stage that the works passed to the Harris Brothers, and consequently became Harrisville, a name which may be found —with a magnifying glass— on today's maps. The transfer did little good, however, for Harrisville went by the board at a sheriff's sale in 1891, and was abandoned about 1893. A fire razed the entire village in 1914, and most of the naked walls were soon reduced to rubble. Today Harrisville stands not unlike a Roman ruin, its old walls rising impressively above a mellow-grassed field. The great arched windows of the mill look out upon nothing more than a few willowy cedars that stand sentinel on Barnegat's industrial acropolis.

Plain Salt Hay Again

The market for salt hay, it would seem, was less than a stable affair. In 1824, eight tons were delivered at a Captain Carlisle's landing for $28. The following year, 1825, the same delivery brought only $3, something of a comedown. The price was at $3 for each ton in the 1840s, free-on-board[6] twenty-ton barges. The railroad depot in Manahawkin sometimes handled a hundred tons of hay a week in 1906, and it brought $7 a ton when delivered baled. An agent would stand alongside the loading platform with a scale and hook each bale, totaling the amount for payment.

[6]Without charge to the buyer for goods placed on board a carrier at the point of shipment.

However, the market began a precipitous decline with the introduction of the automobile, which put livestock in a marginal position. Coupled with this, an extensive state program to ditch the marshes for mosquito extermination permitted a vast influx of fiddler crabs, which honeycombed the sedge with their burrows. The spongy tunnels made passage for mule teams unsafe, despite their mud-boots, and the ditching itself made large, unbroken areas of marsh uncommon.

A 19th century salt-hay scow. With such windage, the craft must have been poor performers to windward... if they could tack at all! Notice how the goosenecks on the main and forebooms are allowed to slide up the mast to make provision for the massive deck cargo.

Charlie

Charlie Weber was probably the last man to cut hay in the Barnegat area, and surely the last to do so in the Mullica basin. He began his career in the early 1890s, and by his second season was cutting five hundred tons a year. This was the product of tracts hundreds of acres in extent and a mile across at some points. The annual custom was to hold auction for the rights to cut over the marsh, rights going to the man who bid highest.

The Weber barge was better than 40-feet long and could carry fourteen or fifteen tons of hay. There were two crude cabins erected auspiciously at opposite ends of the deck, one for Charlie and the other for the teams. The entire barge was towed by an ancient and gasping power garvey. Charlie cut hay well into postwar years, despite his own advancing age, cutting some fifty or sixty acres a season, his equally aged team plodding along in their mud boots and draped in sacking to shield them somewhat from the onslaught of a vast mosquito population. Strangely enough, in spite of industry-wide conditions, Charlie was getting $14 a ton in the early 1940s.

One can still get salt hay these days, its chief use being mulch for gardens and construction. Most of it apparently comes from marshes along the Delaware. Charlie Weber was "in the groove" when he maintained that automobiles "ruined everything for always." The marshes around our bay lie peaceful and bear their crop annually in vain. The bones of an occasional scow rest worm-riddled in quiet creeks or cast up to bleach on a lee shore.

Ye Cranberry

Cornelius Weygandt said that the cranberry submits to cultivation but retains the wild savor that it is its birthright. Even in bogs like those once found near old Cranberry Inlet, tiny patches of berries grow amongst the dunes, springing up in swales and hollows, where a covering of green moss bespeaks sufficient moisture for their sustenance. The previous season's berries often survive the entire winter in quite edible condition, frequently encased in a snow-filled depression over which sand has drifted, insulating it from the spring sun until late March. One author details a delightful practice; hiking through the dunes with a tin of sugar and lunch, stopping behind some gale-sculpted shelter to brew up cranberry jam on the spot.

But winter's moisture has softened the hard seed within each berry and with the warming trend, it sends out a tiny rootlet, which is followed, in time, by a runner with erect green leaves. In June, mature plants produce an insignificant pink flower that develops into the familiar berry. Rarely, a berry will get as big as an inch across, but most are considerably smaller. Towards autumn they take on their crimson hue and can be considered ripened by September or October.

Cranberries are a member of the heath family and a similar species is common to the Netherlands, where they are a staple in the diet of cranes; hence, we are told, the word "Crane-berry." Of course, the Indian gathered these fruits prior to the European, although the latter soon adopted the habit of foraging, and are known to have sought cranberries as early as 1680. There is, however, no record of cultivation before 1840. Popular legend attributes the first attempt at doing so to "Peg-leg" John J. Webb, who purportedly began by pushing the vines into a soft-bottomed bog with his wooden limb. This, we are told, was in 1845, and John made $35 a barrel that season, selling the berries to ship chandlers who eagerly sought them as an antiscorbutic. Actually, the wooden leg wasn't John's secret of success; rather it was that he hit upon the idea of controlling the bog's water level so that it could be flooded in winter, protecting the plants both from frost and many the diseases to which they were subject.

According to Henry Charlton Beck, the "true" berries were upland growth, and are divided into two main classes; "boggies" and "staggers," the reference of which I can only hypothesize as meaning grown in bogs or wild. At any rate, subsequent agriculturists applied the basic principles of water control as expounded by old "Peg-leg," and kept between 2- and 9-feet in depth over the plants from flooding in November, until about the tenth of May, when drainage was made. Examination proves that "Peg-leg" Webb's early precautions were vital to the industry's obtaining an economic foothold. The worst plague the plants suffer is "false-blossom," which is spread by the diminutive leafhopper. Fungi such as scald, blast and rot are also detrimental, as are a number of insects: yellow and black-headed fireworms, cranberry girdlers, and grasshoppers. How glad the plants must be when the water saves them from such hosts!

The cranberry suffers also from a unique microclimatic situation that makes their habitat especially cold on still autumn nights. First, the natural moisture uses up much of the sun's heat daily to evaporate rather than warm the ground, thus leaving the bog soil considerably cooler than its surroundings by nightfall. The fact that bogs are naturally depressed, and usually surrounded by higher growth or embankments, makes them veritable refrigerators. Professor Vaughn Haven, of the Rutgers Department of Meteorology, reports a night in September, 1958, when the temperature at 5 feet above ground was a seasonable 40°F, and 2 inches above the bog floor it was an icy 12° F.

Economics

A boon in cranberries made them popular as a local crop. By 1850, virtually everyone had a bog of his own, but, by late in the 19th century, the per-acre value of bog land dropped precipitously to a dollar. There was still enough return to keep the industry going, however, even if only on a marginal basis. The incentive must have indeed been great enough, for the cost of preparing the bogs alone was $1100 an acre in the 1880s. First, the land had to be cleared and burned free of all growth, then ditched for drainage, a dike erected for flooding, and a cover of sand spread 2- to 4-inches deep. Cuttings of young vines were pressed into this 6-inches apart, in rows spaced 16 inches. It took four more years before the floor was covered and the plants producing well. By this time, however, such a bog might be providing an annual income of $900, although $800 was more a typical value. Perhaps a function of the times, we find in the 1930s only some ten percent of suitable bog area was under cultivation.

Following the spring drainage, there is virtually no maintenance to a bog, except the recent practice of chemical dusting, which affords additional protection to the plants while they are exposed. There is no regular weeding, cultivating or fertilization to be done. When the crop ripens, local Pineys[6] are called in to begin picking.

[6]*Denizens of the Pines*

Chances are they have already been making forages into the bogs prior to this, moonlighting a few bushels for their own accounts, and letting them ripen out back of the cabin.

Picking proceeds for four to six weeks until it is time for a single weeding, which prepares the bog for the next season. By then, it is November and the bogs are flooded for the winter. Occasionally the bogs will be flooded to a shallow depth during a cold snap, as such would frostbite the vines.

In the early days cranberries were picked by hand, a rather laborious process to say the least. Then a bright chap named Robert Ford introduced a basket and cloth-covered paddle that greatly speeded the situation. A toothed scoop was devised soon afterward by an unknown genius in Green Bank. This device consisted of a hollow, box shaped scoop, the lower leading edge of which was serrated with long comb-like wooden teeth. Controlled by a handle on top, it was swept through the vines, which passed between the teeth, leaving the berries behind. With the scoop, a picker could take two, and even four bushels in a five or six hour period which, at forty cents a bushel, let the poverty-bound Piney earn possibly $8 a day. Not too bad, one must confess, especially for 1878.[7]

[7]*Modern harvest is done with the bogs flooded, the berries loosened mechanically, following which they float and are gathered.*

More recently, to quote figures published in 1958, the New Jersey bogs have produced an average of 90,000 one-hundred pound barrels a season. We consequently rank third in the nation as producers of the berry, behind Massachusetts and Wisconsin, which together turn out a vast 850,000 barrels a year. Our berries are marketed through cooperative associations that serve primarily the east coast.

Marl

Agricultural pursuits of other natures have never had particularly great significance in the economy of the Barnegat area. West of Toms River and Manahawkin, there are areas with relatively fertile soil that have supported a degree of dairy farming and the cultivation of corn, and other vegetables. Even some potato production has been carried. Still, figures indicate that there has been relatively little activity in these fields over the years. In 1850 there were 26,400 acres of farmland in Ocean County; in 1890, 31,775 acres; and in 1900, 34,800 acres. We are told that the amount declined somewhat during the first half of the present century. One flaw of the region as an agricultural area may be that it lies south of the normally more fertile marl belts, which touch it only in southern Monmouth and northwestern Ocean counties.

Marl represents ancient sedimentary deposits remaining from a vast prehistoric sea that covered our state during the Cretaceous period. Pockets of marl are often rich in their yield of fossils, but their greatest value lies in the decomposed shell and green sand that make up the greater part of their bulk. An advertisement in 1899 says of a New Jersey marl-pit:

> These Marl Beds have had a reputation for the superior quality of its Marl. Over 4% of Phosphoric Acid.

Its use, historians record, was first suggested by Peter Schenck, an Irish worker at Marlboro in 1768, but the period of its greatest employment extended from 1830 to 1870. During the 1830s there were considerable diggings along the Manasquan in Howell Township and near there, a rail spur was built in 1853 to carry it. Marl was broken from the earthy beds with a fork and the bulk of it was carried in horse-drawn wagons to local fields. After 1875, it was largely replaced as fertilizer by (bird) guano, bone-dust, superphosphates, and later by the standard-formula industrial products.

Marl was taken commercially, however, as late as 1937, from a bed on Route 70 near Marlton, for use in water softeners. The yield was about a thousand tons per acre and sold for some $100 a ton. It was screened of the grosser impurities and then re-screened before being pressed into bricks.

The Livestock

There was a time, you know, when New Jersey was untouched as a sheep-raising locale. In fact, a census, taken just before the Revolution showed no less than 143,000 of the woolly beasts in residence. The coast was hardly unproductive in this venture; sheep were grazed in great numbers on the isolated barrier beaches. As late as 1876, Island Beach had a population of several thousand. The only apparent problem was that wind-whipped sand became imbedded in their coats, and, so laden, they were unable to walk home.

Recalling our Quaker lad, David Mapes, who tended cattle on Squan Beach after the Revolution, we note another endeavor early seized-upon by coastal residents: wintering their livestock on the beaches which served as natural corrals, virtually free from natural predators such as bear, fox and wildcat, which lingered in the pines until the 1800s. There were even some horses raised on Long Beach Island.

The settlers treated the barrier beaches as common land for many years, even though the original English deeds were still technically valid. They ferried cattle back and forth each year for a while, but soon a few began evading the roundup and, eventually, most were left there to run wild. It is said that some of the brown cattle were castaways from a wrecked ship, but it appears that this is unsupported romance and not backed up by anything factual.

At any rate, the herds were there almost continuously for a period of two hundred years, and reached such a state of incivility as to menace intruders amongst the dunes, especially when calves were being sought for branding. Many years ago they were even hunted, much as one would go after water buffalo. By the 1880s, the last herd on Island Beach was down to about thirty head. The remnant met a sad but colorful end through a wild gun-and-horse-back chase, during which all were driven from the dunes and exterminated.

They left their mark, however, in two centuries of grazing — there were countless strange growths and natural grafts from chewed trees and shrubs, which were of interest to naturalists some years ago. And, another mark: In 1927, a full-moon tide cut back a dune on the north end of Tucker's Beach, tearing away a 10-inch layer of ancient peat to lay bare the bay mud beneath. There, perfectly preserved, was the hoofprint of a wild cow, over a century old, yet clear as the day bossy wandered by.

A final reminiscence on livestock came from an old sphagnum moss-gatherer, who, in 1937, told how a generation before, the Forked River "mountains" were thronged with wild pigs, branded and released by Pineys. The father of the moss-gatherer used to fill his pockets with corn to entice the leaders home with him. The sows and their newborn piglets followed docilely.

Ever since colonial times, rare has been the household that didn't have at least a few chickens. Now, since the turn of the century, New Jersey, largely the Pines, has found herself advantageously situated between the egg-hungry markets of New York and Philadelphia. Accordingly, the state-wide chicken industry, representing $100 million in capital and some 18 million chickens has evolved. In 1958, Rutgers University reported that Ocean County was rated among the nation's top nine poultry counties. In the more developed sections we find the feathered creatures ensconced in modern, multileveled, air-conditioned palaces, which house countless thousands of birds apiece.

Unfortunately, poultry is presently suffering a fate analogous to that of the textile industry: there are just too many sellers entering the market, driving the price ever lower. Eventually, those who, without economies of scale, are unable to compete, approach extinction. Unionization, however, had crept in as of 1960 and, while I cannot see this as a valid solution, only time will tell.

Some Observation

Looking back over the two centuries of European habitation, it is quite clear that the Barnegat area has shifted from one endeavor to another, each subsequently yielding to something else. In many ways this is far from a distortion occasioned in the telling. A possible reason for this lies in the very soil which, by nature, is not conducive to extensive cultivation. Without agriculture the region remained relatively primitive and population tended to emigrate toward the later industrialized areas to the north and west.

But along the sea, a new and unifying trend was apparent from the 19th century onward: the resort industry. This endeavor created a vast demand for easy access to the shore, culminating in such arteries as the Garden State Parkway. Access came at a propitious moment. With the trend toward decentralization of industry, the numerous persons fleeing the metropolitan complexes found increasing opportunity for employment in their new home territories. Still, a greater proportion used the roads and commuted north to work, as job opportunity was not keeping pace with the growth of permanent population. Brick Township saw her population soar from 4,319 persons in 1950 to 13,282 in 1959. Ocean County as a whole has logged a 70.4 percent population increase during the decade 1950-1960.[8]

Industry, meanwhile, has made hopeful incursions into more rural areas such as this; attracted not only by a surplus labor market but also easily obtained land and a good supply of ground water, which has been a subject of great shortage in more metropolitan sectors. Hardly incidental is the fact that people and governments alike welcome new industry both as employers and as tax-buffers against rising school and municipal costs.

In 1959, a new frontier was hinted at: mineral resources. Extensive ilmenite deposits were unearthed north and south of Lakehurst. The mineral — a titanium-bearing metal of extraordinary lightness, strength and corrosion resistance — is found in local sands, and used in pigmentation as well as the manufacture of paper and rubber. Thus far, it has been found in only five states, with the extensive beds in Florida perhaps being equal to the New Jersey deposits. The ore is extracted by a complicated and expensive dredging process, in which all but two to three percent of the material bulk is returned to the ground. There is consequently no scarring of the land.[9]

A wise move was made by the state in 1954, when it acquired the vast Wharton Tract that comprises a great percentage of the Mullica basin area. The purchase, some 96,000 acres, was made for $3 million and looks far into the future of expanding populations by reserving some 2.5 percent of the state's land area as a potential water supply. It can yield some 300 million gallons a day, and possibly as much as a billion.

But let us return to the sea, that being a more fitting setting for our story, and one in which I am more comfortable. That great, sometimes lolling, sometimes furious creature has yielded a living for coastal people for many centuries.

[8]The vicinity of Barnegat Bay (more than just Ocean County) reached 392,000 people in 1990. Brick Township alone had about 67,000 people in 1990. The region was growing at a rate of 98,000 people per decade.

[9]After a long subsequent career in coastal and estuarine ecology, the author disavows his youthful enthusiasm about population growth, economics development and the extraction of mineral or natural resources in this chapter. The condition of Barnegat Bay and her watershed, forty years after Closed Sea was written, strongly supports this disavowal.

Chapter 10

From the Sea

The Salt Harvest

Over the centuries of recorded history, salt has played a significant role in the story of man. Christ said: "You are the salt (preservation) of the earth but if salt has lost its taste how shall its saltiness be restored?"[1] Caesar's African legions were paid a "salarium," which they could barter for whatever they chose, be it a material good or the favors of a local girl. During the Middle Ages, salt was one of the few commodities that sustained the bare thread of commerce that wound through the post-Roman economic decay. Its value in certain primitive areas is demonstrated in that, even today, twelve straw containers of salt will purchase a wife in Sierra Leone, West Africa.

We touched on the Revolutionary role of salt in the American colonies, but the story is far more lengthy. Since England considered the commodity on her list of forbidden manufactures, it was extracted only by a few small and isolated contraband works until the 1770s. But with the onslaught of the Revolution, there was an immediate and desperate need of salt as a food preservative both at

[1] *Sermon on the Mount, Matthew 5:13.*

sea and ashore, and as a factor in explosives production. Along the Mullica, I am told that it was even formed into blocks for use as currency, which though blackened after changing hands innumerable times, retained its value where printed Continental currency fluctuated often to disastrous extremes. New Jersey found itself in a questionably enviable position, being virtually the only producer of salt in the colonies. Consequently, the coastal works drew the attention of General Washington; a letter to General Forman, dated October 19, 1777 states:

> GenL Forman
> Sir;
>
> (The) salt works...are so truly valuable to the public, that they are certainly worth your attention...
>
> > I am sir
> > Yr most Obt Sev
> > G. Washington

The result was a little-known campaign in Monmouth County, which during that period included territory South to Egg Harbor. It was not long after the commencement of hostilities that, despite some controversy in the state legislature, the salt works were granted draft exemption for one laborer per five hundred gallons boiling capacity.

Just inside Cranberry Inlet, along the bay shore north of the Toms River mouth, the marsh is indented by what is today called Goose Creek. Here, Thomas Savadge erected a salt works with a £400 appropriation voted him by the Pennsylvania Council of Safety. The location and works were titled the Coates' Point Works, after a Philadelphia merchant who maintained an interest in the establishment. The Continental Congress later appropriated an additional £6,000 for expenditure at the works in view of their significance.

Following Savadge's death, the works were advertised for sale in the *Pennsylvania Packet* on November 9, 1779. They were then represented as having some fifty acres of land, "commodious" buildings, which included a dwelling house, boiling house, drying house, two storehouses, a smithy shop, a windmill with pumps, and something identified only as "etc., etc." which no doubt hid a multitude of sins. The remains of these structures were said to be visible as late as 1850 but have long since been swallowed by housing developments in the area — the unfortunate Thomas Savadge laid to rest since October, 1779, the works now came under the ownership of John Thomson of Burlington.

The Modus Operandi

Coates Point's windmill and pumps were used to draw fresh brine to the "saltern"; a wooden shed where it was boiled over hot wood fires, which consumed vast quantities of cordwood. To conserve fuel, the broad iron pans[2] were often left in the summer sun to allow the process to proceed by more economical evaporation. Movable sheds were set over the heavy pans during inclement weather. The resulting product was a heavy paste of salt which was scooped into "sugar loaf" shaped baskets and hung up to dry.

Depending on the location, various methods were employed for concentration of the brine as it came from the sea. The Cranmers and Ridgways of Barnegat owned at least two of the three works operating there during the war. They looked for a spot in the marsh where vegetation was sparse, indicating a high salt content in the moisture there. A trench was dug and, as the brine seeped in, it was ladled out and boiled in vats over arched ovens. Others would erect sluice gates across the thorofares between marshy islands, closing off these "slews," as they called them, and allowing the sun to effect such concentration as was possible. A similar method was found in the intricate networks of plank troughs erected at other establishments.

In addition to the works mentioned at Toms River and Barnegat, there were others to the north at Wreck Pond, the Manasquan, and the Metedeconk. To the south, there were Brown's Works at Forked River, Newlin's Works at Waretown, and probably, during the Revolution, facilities at Tuckerton. In addition it is probable that there were a number of small establishments of a less permanent nature along the sea.

A salt works produced between five hundred and eight hundred bushels a year, each bushel weighing about fifty-five pounds. They were shipped inland aboard wagons, often under guard by the Continental militia, to various markets where a bushel brought three pounds, ten shillings.

Even disregarding wartime disruptions, tending the vats was not without discomfort; workers were broiled by summer sun, baked by the boiling fires, and attacked fiercely from all quarters by hordes of the dastardly Jersey mosquito. At Great Egg Harbor, on August 11, 1780, Thomas Hopkins wrote:

> We arrived (at the Salt Works) at six o'clock through Shoals of Musquetoes althe (sic.) way who attacked us on every quarter with great Venom...Three Wood Cutters at the Works...came in and said they could not stand it any longer, the Musquetoes being so very thick....

And, on August 24, a few miles north at Tuckerton, the Hopkin's Works were having trouble getting meat for their bellies: "N.B. : Broach'd our last barl Poark." But, it was soon noted: "Bot a Bull of Jaffett Leads (Japeth Leeds, who apparently had a few left after the British had been through.) for eight pounds hard money." The bull, we are informed, weighed four hundred pounds, and the "hard money" was no doubt something more substantial than either salt or "Continentals."

Following the Revolution there was still a market for salt in the growing economy until the turn of the century when mined and imported salt all but wiped out business. During the War of 1812, attempts at revival met with some success and, even in 1816, Daniel Thatcher of Massachusetts built new works with a windmill at Tuckerton, the establishment being erected for a cost of $4,000. Still, after 1800, it can be said that New Jersey salt was no longer an important commodity and, in 1844, the insightful opinion was expressed: "This business has gone down."

Thusly did it die, and virtually all that is left can be summed up by a few ancient cast iron salt pans, filled with dirt and weeds, rusting out their days in someone's yard.

Whale Off

A 17th century explorer, David Pieterzen DeVries, cruised offshore in 1635 and, coming upon an immense pod of whales, he "speared" seventeen of them. Recording the event, he became the first whaler to operate, if somewhat informally, off the New Jersey coast.

That was but the beginning, and, by the latter years of that century, Nantucket and New Bedford lads were bringing their boats alongshore each summer. The craft they employed were shoal draft, and the decks were stacked with empty barrels for oil. The crew was of eight or ten. Barnegat Inlet, being so shallow and tempestuous, was bypassed by entering through an inlet "north of Barnegat," which we met in somewhat nebulous form in an earlier chapter. Inside the bay, they set up watches on the sea beach to await their quarry, which was taken from the beach by small boats.

One of the earliest of these pioneers was Thomas Applegate, who received a license to "take Whales & similar great fish" between Barnegat and the east part of Providence, Rhode Island, on February 14, 1678. The fee for such privilege was 1/20 of the oil taken. Early recognition was given to the importance of a nascent whaling industry by London, which, in 1683, instructed Gawen Lawry, Governor of East Jersey to "take particular inspection to the convenience of fishing...lest the fishermen be drawn elsewhere for want of encouragement."

Perhaps not incidentally, in 1690, the first permanent station was set up on Long Beach Island at "Harvest Cedars"[1] near the Great Swamp.[2] Within a few years two more stations had arisen, about three miles north and south of the original, peopled by such families as the Rutters, Cranmers, Mullins, and Stevens. The station a mile south of Harvest Cedars came to be known as High Point.

Pursuit

Whaling brings to mind the classic cry of the bluewater whaler, wrapped about the pitching main-truck of a powerful square rigger: "Blow! She blows! Off the starboard bow!" while the behemoth erupts from a seething cauldron of foam. But that wasn't the cry of a coastal whaler, who preferred the curt: "Whale off"! Not as much color you say? Well, picture the response as six men drive their stout double-ender through an obdurate surf, stroking seaward to close the mammoth prey. Within a scant few yards of the beast, stinking vapor from its blowhole drifting in his eyes, the bow oarsman, or boatsteerer, ships his sweep for a harpoon and plunges 6-feet of iron into the black hulk. A second's lag and the

[1] Margaret Thomas Buchholz, borough historian in 1994, says it was originally called Harvest Cedars after a stand of cedar on the site where salt hay workers quartered.

[2] The Great Swamp once flourished along the bay shore between Surf City and North Beach.

whale sounds, a half mile of coiled manila line screams, smoking, from the wooden tubs and spins wildly into the depths. Then ominous silence while the boat waits for her prey to surface.

The Northern Right whale (so-called because it was the "right whale" to catch) was the most hunted among whalers, for it was docile and easy to catch, and desirable for both its oil and baleen, which was useful in making mi'lady's corset. Another prize catch was the Sperm whale, or *spermaceti*, so named for the case in its head containing a wax-like substance, valuable in the production of smokeless candles and machine oil. The Sperm whale was a dangerous fellow, with heavy teeth on its lower jaw and tremendous crushing tail flukes. The whalemen said, verily, it "fought with both ends."

The Dirty Work

The big whales, say, from 40 to 90 feet, were not brought back to the beach, since, once they were grounded on the bottom, half the blubber would go to waste through inability to turn the carcass over. Such prey were marked by the owner and towed through the inlets where, in quiet water, they were "cut in" while floating. The remains of such an operation, a skeleton, were found in 1915, settled in the mud of a thorofare running between Mordecai Island and the sea beach at Beach Haven, a short way above Egg Harbor Inlet. On the other hand, smaller whales[3] were towed close into the surf and, on the high tide were sweated[4] right through the undertow, where, on the falling tide, they could be flensed for "trying" the rendering of oil from blubber.

If one walks a deserted section of the sea beach, just after sunset, one can imagine easily the flash of flensing knives, the odor, the silhouettes dragging blubber through the shallows reddened with blood for hundreds of yards in each direction. The beach would have glowed with a dozen fires, above which great iron kettles squatted heavy with trying blubber. I think it lacked not for color of any sort.

The Inmans

Aaron Inman and his progeny whaled throughout the 18th

[3] The skeleton of one of the small whales is on display at the Long Beach Island Historical Museum in Beach Haven.

[4] To pull with block and tackle.

century and well into the 19th century. Harvest Cedars was flourishing as a tiny whaling community by 1812 and by the middle of the century, possibly through local dialect, "Harvest" evolved into Harvey. The Inmans, meanwhile, maintained a constant whale watch during the propitious months from a tall pole in the dunes, called an "owl's tree" with pegs alternating as steps and a platform on top. By 1823 there were twenty families at the spot.

It appears that by this time, however, the whales were moving away. Where once the sea was covered by their black bulks, a sighting now became rare. John F. Watson, author of *Watson's Annals*, speaks of a visit to the island in 1833 where Steven Inman, then one of only a dozen persons on the strand, still caught "two or three whales a season," usually in February or March. It was reported that their take was between forty and fifty barrels a season, all of which were rendered in the old manner, amongst the dunes. Just when whaling died out is difficult to say, as no precise information has presented itself to date. A local resident did, however, recall as late as 1914, how his father had assisted in taking two whales off Harvey Cedars during the course of a single day. "Whale off!," no doubt, was a heeded-cry, as long as fortune was kind.

And today? Do these great mammals still frequent our shore? During World War II, I remember vaguely one morning when a few great beasts were shown to me, forging along the horizon, driven close, it was said, by German submarines lurking at sea.

Currently, small fishing boats occasionally encounter whales offshore. And, since whales seem to sicken more frequently in winter, they sometimes are driven ashore dead or nearly so, creating a smell! Sometimes 60 feet long, they present something of a challenge for disposal. Somebody sent eight men with chain saws against one carcass, and they lasted a week before the odor drove them away. Dynamite was used, as much as ninety sticks, on Brant Beach in 1959, sending fifty-pound chunks of rotten blubber 200- feet in the air. One piece smacked into the police chief's car a hundred yards from the beach. But such catastrophes, over the mellowing years, provide the beach with some interesting souvenirs. And, on Island Beach, beneath a seemingly abandoned shack, I once came across a single vertebra nearly 2-feet across. Had it not been so heavy, I fear I might have pilfered it for a footstool!

The Oystermen

Centuries before the white man, our Indian predecessors enjoyed the use of that plentiful bivalve, the oyster. Following their example, the settlers were gathering them by the 1600s. But, by date alone, we cannot deduce why oystering became so prevalent. The coast dweller was faced by an unproductive and inherently depleted soil and thus, agriculture was less than economic pragmatism. This, coupled with an almost proverbial laziness on the part of baymen, prompted increasing attention to the bay where, in a few hours, a week's food could easily be gathered. Whatever was extra was given to a ready-market of outsiders or visiting vacationers.

But, perhaps from a vestige of conscience, or of yearning toward productive farmland, there was an immense carry-over of farming terminology to oystering. We find the oyster "farmer" "cultivating" his oyster "farm," "sowing" oyster "seed," "planting" and transplanting oysters, letting the "ground lie fallow" between "crops," and even going so far as to "fence off his land" with stakes. Once the crop was harvested, the "field" was dragged to clean it. Eelgrass, which tended to crowd out sensitive young oysters, was actually mowed with a genuine "submarine mowing machine."

The oysterman seeded his young, well advanced from the seed stage, by taking small oysters from the actual seedbed where they began life and distributing them over choice areas of clean bottom. In accordance with this fairly recent practice, it is interesting to note that lime kilns, which once were burned every spring, fed by the shells of shucked oysters, have now disappeared. Today the shells are boated out to the oyster beds and spread over the bottom where they provide a sound base for the rising generation of fry to grow upon. Small comfort in this, for the creature is plagued with danger and predators for the balance of his life. He may be suffocated by tide-borne sediment, bored and devoured by a snail or carnivorous sponges, or ripped apart by starfish.

But, for countless years, the oyster has managed to get by and present a great edible crop each year to the gatherers. An old law once forbade the taking of oysters in months which didn't contain an "r." Basically it was thought that the meat was unsafe during the summer, but a more objective look at the situation reveals noth-

5Dinoflagellate
species can produce
toxins which result in
cases of human
paralytic shellfish
poisoning, though I
know of no such case
in the Barnegat Bay
area, where there are
few oysters at present
in any event.

ing toxic involved. During the early summer however, say in May, when reproduction takes place, the meat may not be of as high quality. There is possibly also the factor that an oyster, during certain periods of the summer, may ingest species of unpalatable protozoans.[5]

Perhaps for these reasons, the bulk of oystering is done in the cooler months, and hence, those containing an "r." The oyster was most frequently collected by tonging, using the scissor-like oyster tongs, consisting of two jaws with eighteen teeth on each, about 35-inches wide, attached to a pair of long poles. Standing in the stern of a little garvey, the bayman would drift slowly over the beds, probing carefully with the tongs until he hit oysters. Grasping firmly, he would haul up his prize, and a heavy chunk of the bay bottom, too.

Moving to the more commercially successful oysterman, we find him using the low-slung dredging sloops. They were modeled closely after the sloops (skipjacks) used in the Chesapeake, with raking masts and marconi-headed rigs.[6] The old days saw many such craft dragging their 4- to 6-foot dredges across the beds, laden nearly to their low gunwales with booty. In the 1880s, the oyster brought some $310,000 in business to the Jersey shore, one of the larger centers being located in Tuckerton.

The oysters were boated to port where they had to be shucked by hand, a process that had been reduced to quite a science. Imagine the familiar figure gracing the Nabisco "Oysterette" cracker box — a gnarled chap squinting down at his little knife — the real operator, however, had a special table, in which an erect blade was set. Directly below was an opening and a bucket. The shucker would strike the blade with the oyster and, miraculously, the shells would fall away through the hole and the meat pop neatly into the bucket. Thus could the expert turn out some 3,500 oysters a day. Long ago, the unshucked — and still living — oysters were packed into old sheet-top or, as they became known, Egg Harbor wagons, and trundled to market over speedy sand roads behind a somnolent mule or ox.

By 1899, most of Barnegat Bay had been informally staked out and planted with either local or "imported" Virginia oysters. In those years the bay had some 296 acres of producing beds. Still, it was not until 1902, when a government act permitted the leasing of underwater rights, that the industry was placed on firm eco-nomic footings. Following that, it became a mainstay for the re-gion, even more so when, many years later, the old sail-dredging laws were repealed, allowing for the first time, the use of engines in the trade.

Stormy Weather

As recently as thirty years ago, the oysterman was a common sight on the bay but then, for some reason, the oyster became less plentiful, and Barnegat dropped virtually from the scene. During the 1950s, the old Cranmer family still ran their 40-foot draggers out of New Gretna on the Mullica, apparently with enough eco-nomic success to "all drive Cadillacs," as one of their relatives put it — a little wistfully, I might add! But that was in Great Bay; Barnegat Bay remained on the obscure side.

Why? Some said it was the Bay Head-Manasquan Canal that had altered the salinity, but it would seem that this slight change would have been beneficial, even for the sensitive oyster. More likely, it was the cumulative lack of tidal circulation, especially through shallow Barnegat Inlet, that harmed the delicates with overly brackish waters, silting, and even a degree of stagnation.[7]

[7]The author now attributes this decline to over-harvesting, the eventual pollution of the bay, and introduced diseases — if the Chesapeake is any model.

Oystering was still a $4 million industry in the state, centered mainly in the Delaware. In 1958, there were beds totaling 35 thou-sand acres. Then, about a year, later a serious and puzzling oyster plague began killing off countless millions of oysters in the Chesa-peake and Delaware areas. Barnegat Bay's oysters have always taken longer (five to six years) to reach marketable size, but the plague, creating a demand for seed oysters, led to the leasing of 450 acres from the state in 1959. Perhaps in hopes that some of the opti-mism would rub off, the bottom near Goodluck Point, Toms River was selected and planted with clamshells. The harvest in that year was less than anticipated due to an exceptional freshwater runoff in July that disrupted spawning.

Indicative of the situation's seriousness, the Delawares River's oyster seedbeds were closed to all takers in September, 1959. The State Commissioner of Conservation and Economic Development extended the order to Barnegat Bay and all other "natural oyster seed beds in New Jersey's tidal waters... until further notice" late in

[8] This "plague" on oysters was discovered by Dr. Hal Haskin at Rutgers University and named at first "MSX," later receiving its scientific name Haplosporidium nelsoni. This devastating parasite is still not understood and only now are "resistant" oysters being developed with some success.

the winter of 1959-1960. Research, at this writing, has still not fully fathomed the causes of the oyster plague[8] but it is hoped that some solution will rescue this savory industry from oblivion.

Clamming

Running a close parallel to, but suffering no such fate as the oyster industry, is the pursuit of clamming. The object of this endeavor is another bivalve that leads a somewhat less sedentary existence than its counterpart, pulling itself back and forth through the sediments with its bulbous foot. Blunt's *American Coast Pilot* of 1887, an otherwise solemn document, extols the clamming to be had in Great Bay and, long before that, the creature found favor with the palates of countless Lenape.

Seekers during the 19th century employed the method called treading to turn up the elusive bivalves. Effectively, one slogged through the black, odorous muck of a tidal flat in bare feet until contact was made. The idea was then to shove in a hand and lay hold before the prey burrowed to safety. The more professional treaders, not desiring to soil their hands or possibly expose a tempting posterior to a competitor, developed the trick of grabbing the clam with their toes and sliding it up the leg, where a flip landed it in a bushel basket. Although young girls and women sometimes treaded, it was generally a man's art and the *femmes fatales* were customarily reserved for opening the shells by knife and stringing the meats for drying or sale to what was primarily a local market.

As this market expanded, however, demand exceeded any supply that could be culled from shallow flats, and a method for working deeper areas was found in the clam rake. Mounted on cedar poles, ranging from 10 to 25 feet in length; the head, patterned generally after the one illustrated on the previous page, took two basic forms. For a hard bottom, stout, fully-curved teeth served to cut only a short way

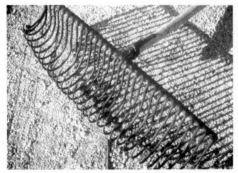

This is a 30-inch wide "chugging" rake, dragged by baymen through the bottom mud to harvest hard clams.

beneath the surface, thus creating a minimum of drag. In a soft bottom, the rake was designed with long, slender, and less curved teeth, allowing a deeper cut with only a comparable amount of drag. On Barnegat Bay, clammers often employed the so-called shinnecock clam rake, the model of which had been imported from Long Island. These had only sixteen teeth, while the local example pictured has three dozen.

Whatever their form, the rakes were used in the operation of "chugging," wherein one or more rakes were trailed on their poles behind a slowly moving boat. The noise of the rake grating over the shell of a clam was transmitted up the pole and served as a signal to pull up. And so were the tastes of clam lovers satisfied, to the tune of 60,000 clams a day in 1890, shipped by the carload from the train depot in Tuckerton.

There are depots today, somewhat outside the mainstream, in Waretown and Barnegat, where the cherrystone and littleneck clams are brought to market. A single buyer here may take up to four million clams a year. And, in addition to this, there is a lively trade between locals and restaurant owners, who no doubt peddle many thousand gallons of chowder a year. Even during the winter, hardy souls will drive a jeep across 12 inches or so of bay ice to saw a slot and grope up a bushel or so of clams, who thought they would be safe for another season.

An Innovation

Offshore exist vast numbers of surf clams, *Spissula solidissima*, which actually live burrowing in the ocean floor, often a day's run out. They gain their title from the fact that, at certain seasons, they are cast dead or dying on the beaches in great numbers, presumably plagued by some disease. These clams are very large, sometimes 7 inches across the valves, and have a large adductor muscle which would be in high favor if the clam did not ingest so much sand with its food. In 1942, draggers off the coast took only 250 thousand pounds of surf clams. A breakthrough in processing by the chowder and frozen food concerns allowed the removal of offending sand, however, and in 1956 the volume had leapt to 11 million pounds annually, representing a value of some $1,212,000 in that year.[9]

[9]At the century's end, most of this catch was landed at Bivalve on the Delaware Bay.

Bay Fishing

The pursuit of a still more elusive denizen beneath the bay's waters is eeling, the craft of catching *Anguilla americana*. It has been said that the true bayman has always had an eel spear. This was used in conjunction with a jacklight that lured the narrow and unsuspecting creature to its mesmerizing beam. There, circling slowly, they met their end by impalement. In winter a mud spear was used, probing through a hole in the bay ice, to bring up hibernating eels.

The eel was also taken commercially, although I doubt the generality of its appeal as a food fish. Still, commercial quantities were taken even in 1956, when the entire state showed a total of 16,793 pounds, with a value of $5,245, or a little over 30 cents a pound.

Some eels have always been taken illegally by dredge,[10] but a far larger proportion come in conjunction with the catching of other species or with a rather ingenious eel trap. This device is a cylindrical wicker basket with a white oak ring woven into the closed end. To this is affixed a length of line bearing an anchoring device and a buoy. At the other end long feathers of wicker are turned in, forming an inward facing cone. These part at the eel's touch and close deftly behind him. Baited with a succulent pulp of horseshoe crab viscera, the trap was irresistible. Numerous accounts tell of the 4-foot long baskets packed so full that no more eels could squeeze in. When they were pulled to the surface, an eager retinue still milled about, yearning to cast away their freedom for a nibble of gore!

Even the little bay scallop has more sense than this — he is collected with a specially designed rake, which has a pocket attached so that the bivalves, more active than their shellfish cousins, cannot bounce themselves to freedom on a jet of water, generated by vigorously "clapping" their shells.

In springs long past, the bayman kept a weather eye on the creeks in late March, waiting for the herring to come in for breeding. Once, they came in phenomenal shoals, nearly blocking smaller estuaries at "cornplanting time when the oak leaves are big as a squirrel's ear." Farmers would stand in the shallows, tossing herring up on the bank to cart away as fertilizer. Later locals, ap-

[10] *A net attached to an iron frame and dragged along the bottom.*

praised of a commercial market for these 10-inch cousins to the shad, sought them with drag nets. They generally waited a few days after the run began, since the early comers were usually young fish.

In the early days of April came the "spawn herring," which often succumbed to gill nets at the rate of one thousand per haul. Gustave Kobbe writes that in 1847, a single catch taken on the Metedeconk amounted to two thousand pounds of fish. It is perhaps not incidental that, to this day, Herring Island, at the mouth of that river, bears a rather appropriate name.

Other locals laid their plans a little earlier than March, erecting a few dozen cedar poles with nets between, naturally, running out from the marsh in a sort of "weir" which culminated in a "pocket," or trap, offshore. The herring, running against this obstacle, would turn away from the shore, swimming along the net, to end their days milling helplessly in the pocket. The young were apparently small enough to slip through the nets or were cast back.

Herring, as well as their relatives, the shad and alewives, suffered greatly from stagnation and pollution in coastal streams and no longer penetrate Barnegat sub-estuaries to any extent.[11] I have seen the weirs set up on occasion, but herring, as such, was not reported in government figures for New Jersey in 1956.

11Dams and culverts on many bay streams block necessary upstream migration for these fish.

Much later in the season baymen turned their efforts to the "fykes," long, bag-like fish traps which were set for snapper bluefish that spend their nascent months in coastal waters before summering in Barnegat Bay. Many of these nets are 5 or 6 feet in diameter, held open by a series of hoops. One on the Manasquan was so large and heavy it had a track made of logs to haul it out for emptying and repair. Some of these nets on the Mullica were taking seven hundred pounds of snappers a year in the late 1930s.

Such comprises a compendium of some, though not all, of the many endeavors, great and small, that have occupied the Barnegat folk over the years. We must, of necessity, now turn to a trade that extends itself a distance off the coast: ocean fishing.

The Pounds

Quite far south along Long Beach Island, cradled amongst the rolling dunes, one may still find the sturdy bows of a few heavy

12The only survivor, as of 2000, is on the ocean side of Route 35, just before the entrance to Island Beach State Park, where a pound boat sits, an emblem for a local restaurant.

wooden vessels, rising proudly against the sky. These are pound boats, remnant of a once extensive fleet that leapt out through the surf every day at dawn, from the middle of April to mid-November, and from Egg Harbor to Sea Girt.[12]

Their nets lay quite a stretch offshore but within the two mile limit, set on poles of North Carolina hickory 70-or 80-feet long and about 75-feet apart. The nets were erected in a long barrier, 1,500- or 1,600-feet in extent, quite like a double-ended arrow. The mechanics are shown quite graphically on the following page. The fish were funneled into a pocket 45- or 50-feet square, the bottom of which could be hauled up to concentrate the catch using lines leading to the surface. It was quite a job as the lads hauled up the heavy, weed-fouled nets inch by inch, sweating them into the boats. As the distance between net and surface lessened, the pocket became a cauldron of seething fish, each thrashing wildly for freedom. Gulls, skirling and dipping all about, often became so engorged at the nets that they had to sit on the water until they had digested some of their meal and could take off. Frequently, the take from a single net amounted to sixty barrels of two hundred pounds each and often the 33-foot boats could come in laden with 25,000 pounds of fish. But, unfortunately, fish were not all that came up with the nets: every two weeks they had to be taken up and freed of seaweed, which invariably accumulated in vast amounts. Sometimes a shark would wander in and become fouled in the mesh, tearing it to shreds in his struggle for liberation. The story is told of a big Swede who caught one such creature thrashing his $5,000 investment to shreds. Enraged, he grabbed a knife and, leaping into the water, dispatched the beast.

I remember, as a little boy, my father dragging me up the beach one morning to watch the pound boats come in at the Manasquan Beach Fishery. The ocean sparkled with traditional brilliance in the early sunlight, silhouetting the heavy boat as she eased in toward the beach. The horses used in hauling the boats up stood quietly at their tackles, and a few men made ready some big wooden rollers on the hard sand near the water.

There wasn't much surf but still the boat moved cautiously lest she swing broadside and roll her rail under, to the final detriment of both boat and catch. The captain waited a moment, engine at idle, dropping over the crest of a wave, then pulled forward to

catch the next. Nose down and yawing[13] just a bit, she came bar-
reling through the undertow and hit the beach. Another wave
caught her transom with a sparkling shower before a line could be
passed through a ringbolt in her stem. Instinctively, the horses
strained forward, the tackles snapped taut, tossing aloft a puff of
dry sand. Ponderously, the laden craft came up the rollers toward
the fishery amid a welter of joking and swearing.

[13]Deviating from a straight course.

The fishermen themselves comprised an interesting, though
unquestionably tough, lot. As well as local men, we find a large
proportion of Danes, Swedes, Norwegians, and some Portuguese,
totaling some twenty to seventy men per fishery. Throw a bunch
of men together like that and you get a colorful group. My uncle
describes Charlie P., a cook, and according to most, not a good
one, for one such coastal establishment. At best a bit short tempered, he managed to control most objections to his somewhat
greasy culinary efforts with a persuasive butcher knife. Appropriately, for the telling at least, the cleaver is said to have once found
its mark. A wild lot they were, but, at worst, they were good fishermen and fine surfmen, proudly relying on generations of experience in the lifesaving service as their legacy of skill.

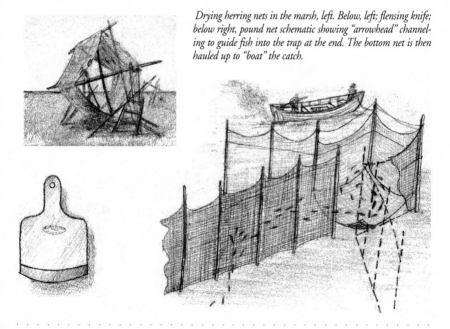

Drying herring nets in the marsh, left. Below, left; flensing knife;
below right, pound net schematic showing "arrowhead" channel-
ing to guide fish into the trap at the end. The bottom net is then
hauled up to "boat" the catch.

The industry was once widespread, with fisheries dotting the shore. On Long Beach Island alone, in 1936, there was the Barnegat City Fishery, Surf City Fishery, the Ship Bottom Pound Fisheries Inc., Crest Fishery, and the Beach Haven Fishery Co. They represented a large capital investment, with some boats costing over $50,000. With $4,000 or $5,000 tied up in the nets, the concerned pound men watched from the beach on stormy days when even their stout boats could not go out. It was at such times that the nets of all longshore establishments suffered dearly.

Problems

One of the greatest problems faced by the pounds is one they can do least about: migration. A large proportion of the edible fish taken in the nets engage in annual migrations — of varying length — for purposes of breeding, or seeking more suitable food or water temperature conditions. Naturally, the factors which determine the intensity, timing, or even the existence of such events are complex and may vary considerably from year to year. This explains both bountiful catches, like the herring in 1847, and the virtual disappearance of tuna from the pound nets. Specimens of this great breed weighing sometimes a thousand pounds, once were found in Beach Haven nets only a mile or so from the beach but have since moved well offshore.

The pounds prospered throughout the first half of the 20th century. At this point, precipitous declines of inshore fish raised havoc with the business and, in 1959, there is only one pound fishery left on the beaches of Long Beach Island where there were five during the thirties. The nets off Manasquan and Sea Girt are worked no longer from the beaches. Boats bound out Manasquan Inlet early each day instead, to return often pitifully unladen. Strangely, as is the caprice of the sea, Manasquan's nets had a fantastic haul in 1947 (one which is still spoken of), when the boats brought in a thousand boxes of butterfish. The fact remains, hard though it be, that the fish must come to the net.

Offshore

Offshore fishing, directly from the boat, modifies somewhat, but only somewhat, the truism just expressed, for at least the trawlers, draggers and seiners can go in search of their catch. But even that takes money. The concept goes back many years, when locals pushed their little catboats through the surf and went to sea with a couple of handlines. However, technology being what it is, one needs more than a catboat or Seabright skiff today.

In 1956, the U.S. Department of the Interior reported that there were 5,298 men engaged in the fishing industry of our state, operating 2,722 watercraft of which 425 were of major size totaling 10,974 net tons. The landings at New Jersey docks in that year were 513.8 million pounds with a total value to our economy of $15.2 million. It's an important business to many people, but not without its complications.

> Dear Boys, ain't you glad
> you never fished,
>
> Never dugged for them
> clams.
>
> Clam(s), folks never used
> when you had 'em,
>
> But hollered for 'em when
> there ain't none.
>
> Oh, dear boys, ain't you
> glad you never fished.

So runs a mournful lament of the Forked River region, recorded for posterity in *Folklore Songs of the United States*. It plucks rather insistently at the essence of supply and demand as presented to the fishing industry.

The vast bulk of catches are taken in summer, when the breeding runs are on and many species come inshore to shallow and warmer waters. So great is the contrast that thirty-four of our state's forty commercial docks close during the winter months. Thus, when Lent rolls around, toward the beginning of each year, and a vast leap in the consumption of fish begins, the finny creatures are just not being brought to market. Demand conversely plummets after Easter, when the early catches are just beginning their spring runs. Moderns quickly counter with a proposal that quick freezing

The purse seiner: A catch of menhaden is drawn in by a large suction hose. The "purse" is set out by small boats and drawn in a circle before hauling.

Draggers (above): There are several old draggers such as this one, converted from a former "Banks" type fishing schooner. Note the small, steadying sail to ease the ship's motion in heavy weather offshore.

Trawlers: The otter trawls are pulled by many types of boats, this model being a popular one in Jersey waters. Detailed is the "door," or rane, which spreads the net properly when towed. Each is about 3 1/2 feet long.

is an answer. The reality of the situation is that sufficient facilities were not possible until recently.

The fisherman has traditionally been a highly individualistic man; the outsider (being) neither "wanted nor needed," as a rule. The mode of organization has remained virtually unchanged throughout centuries past. The boats are often owned on a partnership-basis, or are passed from father to son, thus effectively restricting entry and employment, in large measure, to members of the "fishing families."

A rare communal effort on the part of local fishermen was the erection of cooperative ice houses in the dunes. Tent-shaped, of stacked planking, and packed with insulating salt-hay, they managed to keep at least a little ice into the warmer months, which allowed some stalling of their product's usually rapid decomposition. Still, with the exception of small amounts of dried and canned fish, the bulk of the catch had to be placed quickly on the market or be lost completely for use other than as fertilizer.

Thus, in the lean season, while demand was at its peak, the fisherman (who was in all probability already hurt by low prices during the prolific months) was subjected to long layoffs. If he were an owner, he bore continuing expense while his ship was idle. All too frequently, his finances were insufficient to carry him through, especially if the fish didn't come in the next spring to cover his debts. It has always been a hard life, requiring tremendous courage, a skill on which the fisherman's life might depend, and constant and rigorous exposure to the elements. When he couldn't even make a decent living, spirits must have been low.

The vicious cycle is apparent. The capricious fish requires of his pursuer a wide scope of operations and strong economic position, while he provides evasions and difficulties which exhaust both. On top of this, the fishermen only sell to large processors, who are effectively what the economist would call "monopsonists," a single large buyer dictating price and market conditions to relatively numerous sellers.

The trend that conditions such as this created is obvious. The boats tended toward greater size, whereas previously men worked their little Seabright skiffs (16- to 18-feet long and driven by a tiny sail), dropping a puny handline over the pitching rail. The new craft are ocean-going trawlers, draggers, and seiners ranging from a minimum of 30 to 90 feet, and often over 100 feet in length.

Larger and more seaworthy, they can work well offshore for days at a time and tap the deeper winter migrations near the continental shelf. Basing their operations from the inlet harbors, they are thus permitted year-round fishing. Scores of the little boats still remain, but with their more primitive methodology, they do well only during especially propitious "runs." Nevertheless, they hang on, with the result that a large proportion of the vessels engaged in commercial fishing are classed as "boats: motor and other," a mean length coming to only about 30 feet.

The offshore boats we find are owned now by larger units, the corporation being most convenient, but manned still by the same breed of hardy Scandinavians. The methods they use are basically three in number:

[14]Modern menhaden fisheries use small planes as "spotters," radioing the location of each school.

1. The "purse seiners" sight their fish generally by eye, setting out a long net from smaller boats, which hangs deep into the water suspended on floats at the surface. This is gradually drawn by the little yawl boat in a circle about the school of fish and, its bottom closed by a drawstring much like the purse after which this type of seine is named. The noose is tightened and the fish quite literally ladled out of the resulting pouch into the mother ship's hold.[14]

2. The "draggers" go primarily after bottom quarry, such as surf-clams or scallops. They tow a heavy dredge across the ocean floor scraping up whatever comes in their path. This need not always be fish. Tonnes Anderson was working offshore April 1956, when his ship suddenly lurched to a halt and began careening backwards at a great rate, oblivious to the engine's efforts. Finally, and perhaps mercifully, the cables parted and Tonnes went home without his gear. Four days later, our first atomic submarine, the *Nautilus* surfaced off Groton, Connecticut — with Tonnes' net draped neatly over her huge sail, or conning tower, to use World War II terminology. In 1959, the *Adele*, another craft out of Point Pleasant, brought up the anchor of an old sailing vessel. The ancient hook was 9 1/2-feet long with 300-feet of chain attached, each link of which weighed ten pounds and was stamped "Philad." Coated with deep rust and the growth of many years' immersion, it was a strange relic as it lay beside the *Adele*'s pier. It was believed to be the largest anchor[15] recovered off the New Jersey coast.

[15] The Fortuna's anchor, recovered in 1983 and displayed in front of the Ship Bottom Borough Hall, is 10.2 feet long

3. The "trawlers" also fish the bottom with a wide throated conical net known as an "otter trawl," so called after the door-like

fins that ride on its dual cables to hold the mouth open. They go in search of deep-running school fish, and bottom fish in general.

The offshore boats were accompanied by increasing organization ashore. One of the earliest of such efforts was a refrigeration plant at Beach Haven, where the fishermen pooled their catches for holding until the market was more favorable. Even the old pound net operators made an attempt at modernization when they replaced their poor horses with tractors. With expanded range offered by the new vessels, another means of combating the monopsonistic situation was provided. By radio, the captains could literally "shop" up and down the coast for the best price their catch might bring. Anyone with a short wave could hear them buzzing back and forth (if ungrammatically) at about 2.6 on the marine band.[16]

[16]*Modern marine radio is mostly on VHF wavelengths. Commercial fishermen often talk candidly on channel 8.*

The Fence's Other Side

We have perhaps painted the processors as evil men who exploit the helpless fishermen, but they have been in none-too sound a position themselves. They were, of course on the front line of the disadvantageous demand situation we spoke of earlier. The fact that they often were able to dictate price to their suppliers is tempered considerably by a like truism: that when the price of fish rises, there is generally a tendency for consumers to shift toward meat. Since 1939, a major factor on the cost side of processing has been waste, caused by market demands for better cuts of fish. The biggest shift has been to filets, the boneless slices of meat taken from the fish's side, the balance generally being waste material. This has presented a tremendous problem of disposal in areas of concentrated population, which has all too often been met less than satisfactorily.

A sound concept that has come into vogue since the 1940s is more complete employment of the resources available, creating benefits both in the realm of conservation and cost efficiency. Scraps left behind on the skeleton, when the filets are taken, have been put to use as "fish sticks," which no doubt grace a good proportion of the freezers in our land today. Likewise, valuable fish oil and vitamin products can be extracted from the heads and livers. Cat and dog foods are another employment to which entrails may be

[17] This "by-catch" of
non-target species
contributes, today, to
a serious problem of
over harvesting.

relegated as well as the often considerable take of non-marketable species like the sea robin (*Prionotis evolans*)[17] and so-called "trash-fish."

Fish glue, or "mucilage," is a product made from all wastes when certain of the other processes may be too expensive in relation to the volumes handled. Where oils have been pressed out, a fish meal can be made by grinding the remainder. This has proven most valuable as cattle and poultry feed.

Such processes have become essential because filleting results in a waste of some fifty-five percent of the fish. Still, much potentially valuable material is dumped at sea in greasy malodorous heaps through lack of know-how or funds to initiate new methods. The government seeks to do its share in stopping this through the publication of many pamphlets on processing, which are directed toward the more efficient utilization of the catches brought in.

The Quarry

In April, the sea bass and lobster pots appear on local docks, freshly tarred with their cork and bamboo buoys attached. They soon are cast over the rails of their respective owners' craft to begin the haul.

New Jersey's annual take came to 513,800,000 pounds in 1956, as we said, split up amongst some thirty-five major species of fish and nine major species of shellfish. Summer finds such familiar catches as the porgy, sea bass, five varieties of flounder, whiting and bonita. Winter catches include cod and pollock.

The mackerel was once provider of some $2-3 million in New Jersey, with an historic catch of seventeen million pounds in 1947. Their pattern begins with a spring migration inshore, where they spawn. This activity is subject to many conditions, including the food supply and water temperature. A shortage in fish one season has customarily been the result of a poor breeding period a season or so before.

Mackerel spend the summer inshore, grazing on the greater abundance of food there. With fall, another run is experienced as the fish move offshore for the winter. They are caught by seiners, frequently at night when their feeding excites phosphorescence on the water's surface and facilitates location of the school.

But, modern gear be damned, 1949's catch dropped in 1950 to 250,000 pounds and, in 1951 to only 25,000 pounds. Some amelioration was experienced in 1956, but in general the catches were small. The threat from this failure, and that of other species which moved away, challenged the very existence of many fisheries along the coast, especially those which had not the working capital to widen their scope of operations or withstand the setbacks occasioned using other means.

An Observation

In 1956, this condition reflects not only the capriciousness of the fish but also points up the selectiveness of public demand. Man at present, utilizes only about fifty of the twenty thousand known species of fish. There is a vast resistance to the introduction of a new species on the part of the public. Generally the only way it can be done is to disguise it as a familiar one, at best a poor practice to rely upon. Some of the "tuna" we get today is not tuna at all, though it tastes almost identical and is certainly of equal quality.[18]

[18]Today's global fishery changes much of this 1950s view. Monkfish (Lophius piscatorius), a delicacy now, was once considered an ugly trash fish. Most diners have no idea what a monster they are eating!

The solution adopted by our threatened locals however was not quite of this nature, for they were presented with the prolific menhaden, which is generally considered inedible, although small amounts of it are canned for this purpose.

"That Which Enriches the Land"

Thus was the little 3- to 7-inch menhaden, or mossbunker, called by the Lenape, who spread his oily carcasses on their fields. Strangely, the menhaden itself was nearly a vanished breed around the time of World War I, but in 1956, 463,544,203 pounds of menhaden were landed by New Jersey's three fisheries. This was a large proportion of the total catch for that year, which leaving only about fifty million pounds for edible fish, and the balance for trash fish. Rather a significant factor this wee fellow has become.

Like so many of their fellows, mossbunkers spawn inshore, entering the coastal waters about June, where they act as possibly the most significant food fish for other predators in these waters. The young mature in their third or fourth year. They move about in immense, tightly packed schools, a rather precarious state, forced toward the surface by feeding predators below and driven deeper by screeching gulls and sea birds above. In this state, the schools, often acres in extent, are easily spotted by the seiners that go out in search of them.

How the seiner's purse was set and drawn was explained a few pages back. However, when the poor little fellows are brought aboard, the deed is accomplished by a great suction hose, attached to powerful pumps that draw great volumes of fish and water through a straining device to remove the desired creatures. Apparently a number of unfortunates slip through with the water and are reduced to liquid gore in the pump, emerging as a soup of bloody brine at the discharge pipe. The gulls, and no doubt interested observers from the deep, enjoy it all immensely. The menhaden, by that time, are unavailable for comment.

[19]Crab Island is long closed, with landings being done today in Reedville, Virginia, consolidated into a single company, Omega Protein.

The catch is processed by extremely efficient units ashore, one in the Barnegat Bay area being at Crab Island[19] near Tuckerton. Other segments of the industry might well take heed, as they no doubt are doing, of these processors, who dominate the menhaden trade with a few large chain factories. Countless barrels of oil are extracted from the carcasses to be used by the soap industry, in textile manufacture, paints and varnishes, and plastics, not to mention a surprising employment in aluminum casting. The pulp and meal remaining are put to use as fertilizer and processed as dairy and poultry feed.[20]

[20]Today, menhaden are considered a resource in serious difficulty. The small fish I wrote of in the late 1950s were very young, and likely harvested before they could reproduce at their adult size of 12 to 15 inches.

All this, from the sea, for the benefit of the region and her people, a long economic road from the pound fishery and skiff. For the poetic, they still follow the old ways on Long Beach Island, where the remnants lie, cradled in the saffron-maned dunes with their bows held up to the sky.

Note: Much of the data on commercial fishing in this chapter was taken from a report prepared at Rutgers University in 1959 for oral delivery. Commercial fishing has changed greatly since Closed Sea was written, with one stock after another depleted by ever more efficient gear.

Chapter 11

Rails and Resorts

Opening the Shore

Intrinsic, they say, is the lure of the sea. It has nearly always been so, and Jerseyans of years gone by were no exception in succumbing to this appeal. For my money, there is no greater place to spend a holiday, or any day, than at the shore.

In the 18th century little travel was effected to the shore and that over the most opprobrious roads, if one could classify them as roads! In wet weather, wide-tired wagons blasted deep potholes that rapidly filled with rain and soupy mire; in dry weather soft sand served as a similar hazard. The vehicles themselves added no pleasure to the journey, being at best a uncomfortable stage and more likely an open wagon in which one often had to spend the night. The bone-jarring trip through thick pineland was invariably augmented by hordes of greenhead flies and squadrons of Jersey mosquitoes, whose venomous bite is renowned the world over.

What luxury it must have seemed when the sea was reached, to speed silently over hard sands near the surf, your carriage wheels hardly making an impression! Accommodations, however, still left much to be desired by our standards, as there were but few structures on the sea islands in the early years. Those that were there were rudely built, and furnished with red cedar cut from the island swamps. The Quakers, who settled at Tuckerton in 1699, were known to travel across the bay to Long Beach Island for beach parties as early as 1704, setting a precedent as the first "resort-goers" on the Jersey Shore.

The Railroad

It can safely be said that the first railroad in Ocean County was established by charcoalers early in the 1840s, running some nine miles between Manchester (Lakehurst) area and Cedar Creek, just south of Toms River. Specifically, the track ran from the thundering metropolis of Ong's Hat in the Pines (about one mile northwest of the Four-mile circle on the Pemberton Rd.), to a strategic depot at Double Trouble, on said creek; hence, the Double Trouble and Ong's Hat R.R. Whence cometh such names?

First, there was an early pioneer minister who lived at a spot on Cedar Creek. Here, it seems, his job was to repair the countless muskrat holes that appeared in a mill dam. Once, coming upon two of the creatures busily engaged at the same time he cried in despair: "Here's double trouble!" Locals, amused at his plight let the name stick. How Ong's Hat received its name meets with some dissension. Most probably it comes after Jacob Ong, who traveled regularly north from Egg Harbor in the early 1700s. It was his custom to stop at a cabin he owned in the pines, which may have retained the Dutch designation of a *hoet* (hut). The years could easily have mellowed the name to a most confounding Ong's Hat. It may have been just such confusion that engendered the song about a Chinese cook named Ung, who, by misadventure and Barnegat pirates, was deprived of his precious hat "several hundred years ago."

> They say on windy nights
> the spirit of the cook
> whose name was Ung,
> Still wanders up and down
> the Jersey shore where fate
> his hat had flung.

There's one sandy hill;
Ung's Hat' is its name,
for in that shape it seemed to grow,
Would we find either Ung or his hat
inside? Well, I doubt
if we'll ever know.

— *Folklore Songs of the United States*

And, nicely put by Paul Jones, a journalist:

...if you're down at Barnegat and happen to see a broad brim straw hat... you'll know it's Ung's, and he's looking for it.

Maybe some ghoul with a shovel could settle both questions for us.

At any rate, the Double Trouble and Ong's Hat Railroad was built, its rails of wood, capped with iron. Mule-drawn cars plodded their creaking way from one end to the other. With the advent of steam, some enterprising charcoalers, who ran the affair, imported an iron horse. Setting it proudly on the tracks, they kindled a fire and trundled off... the iron cap curling nicely up behind them from the engines weight!

Writer Harold Wilson reports further on the Manchester-Toms River railroad[1], dating from about 1865-1866, which we may assume traveled approximately the same route as its predecessor. He calls this the first real railroad to that area. Commercial railroads in the main, however, could not conceive of a line ending at the shore. With the resorts that later arose, this might seem folly but then, an isolated, virtually tradeless region, provided little incentive.

But there was still our state's 121 miles of seacoast, 56 of which are in Ocean County, and an increasing demand for efficient transportation to budding recreation areas which already existed at points such as Cape May and Atlantic City. Consequently, by the 1850s, rickety, narrow-gauge railroads wormed their way through the Pine Barrens, and across the coastal bogs, passing in some cases only a few inches above the water's surface.

Strangely, rails to the sea were received with mixed emotions. Lauded by travelers, they were often met with resistance by farmers, whom one would think might welcome swift transport of their goods. They maintained, however, that the engines not only disturbed and often killed their livestock, but that they started fires with sparks from their stacks. They also held that stage and team

[1] *The Manchester-Toms River railroad — mule-drawn — followed the route from Manchester to a spot on the south shore of the Toms River, where the community of Beachwood now stands.*

lines would soon be driven out of business, to the ruination of the hay market on which many of them depended for livelihood. Still, rails did provide a cheap, effective transport for supplies and tourism, shaving days off the laborious journey over unreliable sand trails once faced by visitors and cargo alike.

The knife, incidentally, cut both ways: Those cows the farmer worried so about proved a curse to the railroader in those days before fencing. In time they got used to the trains; in fact, became downright belligerent, standing squarely on the track where no amount of whistle-blowing and hollering could dislodge them. A good many of them were killed thanks to the train's inadequate brakes — never mind that the impact often derailed the engine. How do you get a chunk of iron like that out of a bog and running again?

Speaking of brakes, they were generally so bad that the train was rarely able to stop at the station, having to back up to engage the platform. Also, the cars were joined loosely with short lengths of chain, in such an ingenious manner that even a slowdown would bring the rear cars crashing together, only to yank up tight again when the engine accelerated.

Before coal was generally accepted in the 1880s, wood was the standard and most readily available fuel for steam engines. It was stacked in suitable lengths aboard a roofed tender. When burned, the combustible pinewood oozed hot tar, cast off vast showers of sparks, and dense billows of smoke which were received with consternation by hapless passengers, who could do nothing to escape if the wind were wrong.

Ah! The passenger; well-off indeed, with plenty of fresh smoke to breathe, comfortable board seats upon which to recline and, when he or she wanted off? The helpful conductor would lean out of the car and hurl a piece of wood at the engineer (shouts being wholly futile against the engine's snorting). If his aim was true, the missile found its way past the tender roof, and if the engineer's head was not too callused, a forefinger was elevated, indicating someone wished liberation.

Though the passenger had a relatively rough time of it, we have yet to shed a tear for the poor conductor. People tried incessantly to get their children on free, though the rules said strictly half price. And, railroads were new, a novelty to almost all comers, with a resultant siege of endless and trivial questions to be answered by a conductor already harassed by operational problems. Small wonder that much was written during the period to educate the public in the art and manners of railroad riding — most of it propounded in desperation by the railroads themselves.

Service to the Shore

Those first shaky rails crossed Toms River ground in the 1840s but we must offer credit for the first true long distance haul to the southern coast to the line between Camden and Atlantic City. That, however, is out of our territory.

In 1872, Mr. Archelaus R. Pharo induced the Pennsylvania Railroad to extend a spur as far east as Barnegat, making that the pioneer line to our region. Pharo subsequently purchased the old steamer *Barclay*, which formerly had run across the Delaware between Philadelphia and Rancocas Creek, putting her into the run from Manahawkin to Long Beach Island. He later replaced her with a new vessel, the steamer *Pohatcong*, which ran until the mid 1880s.

The Long Branch and Seashore Railroad followed with service to the coast, pushing southward to the north bank of the Manasquan in 1876. Shortly thereafter, a rail causeway spanned the river, and was described, in 1882, as "a stupendous structure..." over which trains passed "every few minutes." Thus, when Bay Head was incorporated as a borough in 1886, it was the southern terminus of the New York and Long Branch.

In 1880 construction of a bridge by the Pennsylvania Railroad, at Seaside, from Goodluck Point to the beach, interrupted the course of the famed Toms River Cup Race for catboats, which had been sailed since 1871. The rails crossed the bay in 1883 and were extended north to meet the Long Branch, completing service to the upper bay area, and opening the northern sector of Island Beach for development.

Meanwhile, during the mid-1880s, Pharo's steamer received competition when the Pennsylvania pushed another spur across Barnegat Bay at Manahawkin to Long Beach Island. Once across, the tracks of a narrow gauge line were extended south to Beach Haven and north to Barnegat City, on the turbulent inlet. The polished little engine, a Baldwin, I believe, was an eye-catcher for the growing tourist trade, and long the pride of the Manahawkin and Long Beach Transportation Company which owned her. But, no sooner had full service to the beaches been attained, than a cloud appeared on the economic horizon; the days when people took excursion trains to the shore were numbered.

The Auto

The auto came more slowly to these isolated regions due to poor roads and the nature of the economy. Nevertheless, the Manahawkin causeway was opened in 1914 by the Long Beach Turnpike Company. Built of plank on pilings for $90,000, a further bill of $107,000 extended a gravel road along the island and facilitated a merger of this system with the mainland roads. The railroad on the beach, once the only effective mechanized transport available, was abandoned to the gas buggy in 1923, when the tracks and ties were taken up forever.

This, however, was but symptomatic of the larger scene, for improved roads began to creep toward the shore from all directions. With the rise of the family automobile, backed by more reliable engineering that made long-hauls possible, the railroads found their tourist and excursion trade crumbling. There were just not enough bulk cargoes left to pay maintenance on the long spurs leading to the sea. The Pennsy was losing money on the Seaside branch before 1924, but hung on a few years while its application for discontinuation of service was kicked about. Subsequently, the track north to Bay Head was torn up, leaving a station or so to be used mainly as billboards. The bridge was cut out, only a stump remaining at each end. It operated at a profit later under the title Barnegat Pier.[2]

[2] The resulting right-of-way real estate has been worth millions of dollars in the 20th century.

A factor in the death of rails to the sea was an attempt by the Pennsylvania R.R. to adapt its schedule to the needs of commuters. Local farmers refused to milk their cows an hour earlier in order to ship by rail, and milk was the chief freight item to Philadelphia in those days. Trucks, which had been introduced during World War I, snapped up the trade. Since their schedules were far more flexible, they put that branch of the Pennsylvania R.R. out of commission.

The Long Branch has hung on to date. Its terminus once again a turnabout at Bay Head. For some reason, it remained a last stronghold of steam, while diesels captured virtually all other roads, and was consequently visited by shutterbugs and railroad fans seeking to glimpse the dying iron horse. Today, the steamers are gone and a few diesels offer token service to the area, tapping a predominantly commuter trade. The Pennsylvania -Trenton branch, which comes in at Manasquan, is used by only one train daily, and a petition went before the Public Utilities Commission in 1959 to demolish the Broad Street station. With an eye to its decaying nature, the borough hoped there would be no delay.

The Open Road

The auto, meanwhile, as all know, became a problem in its own right. Resorts, developing mushroom-like — or should we say toadstool? — each year drew increasing hordes to the coast. Vastly improved road systems, with such arteries as Routes 9, 34, and 35, plus comfortable, reasonably-priced cars, gave a recreational safety valve to intensifying urban areas like New York and Philadelphia.

Within my short memory, and primarily in the post war boom, the weekend and holiday flow seriously clogged these arteries. Perhaps the greatest single approach to this problem was the toll-supported Garden State Parkway, which runs the state's entire length. On a more limited, but nonetheless critical, scale, was the project replacing the 1914 Manahawkin causeway, which with its slow operating drawbridge, had become known as the "old traffic snarler." The new causeway was completed in 1958, and, in the same year, the old wooden derelict was torn up. Its heir is an impressive structure, visible as far north as Barnegat Inlet. It stretches two miles with a main span of 2,400 feet and a clearance to the bridge deck of 60-feet, designed to eliminate the draw which proved such a burden on motorist and boatman alike. Incorporated for illumination was the latest in fluorescent lighting; eye-level elements, set in the railing to produce, according to an observer, brightness equivalent to "noon, close up." Erected at a cost of $12 million, its salutary effect on traffic flow to the island was immediately apparent.

The first auto bridge to the islands, however, was erected at Seaside in 1913. It was built on pilings and wooden supports cambered to lift crushing bay-ice. This was replaced by the Thomas A. Mathis Bridge, completed in 1950, with an improved approach some years later. An old bridge traverses the bay at Mantoloking, resting on wooden piles that I have regarded with (perhaps unwarranted)[3] suspicion since the collapse of a similar structure over the Manasquan River about 1946. Since about 1958 increasing efforts have been made to meet rising traffic , especially in the upper bay area, with a regionalized approach to vehicle flow, rather than probably less efficacious local attempts. It would seem, for the present, that congestion is keeping pace rather closely with solutions. Gazing upon, or entangled within, a bumper-to-bumper serpentine traffic jam some steaming afternoon, one wonders if progress has been made at all! But then, that easily attained is not dearly cherished.

[3] The same pilings carry weight-limited traffic in 2002.

Resorts

So, it appears, the first vacationers were Quakers from Tuckerton, and possibly Philadelphia, who sojourned around 1704. Moving on a few years we find Tucker's Beach taking the honors when a chap named Reuben Tucker bought that land, from Long Beach south to Little Egg Inlet (then Old Inlet, of course) in 1745. Reuben, in 1765, opened his home for the "health and entertainment of pleasure seekers." Five hundred feet from the shore, Tucker's one-storied structure stood elevated pleasantly on a platform of sand and shells. A well-known, and apparently durable place, Tucker's was still in business in 1823, fifty-eight years later.

It was not long before the idea caught on, with the opening of Horner's boarding house (later becoming the Philadelphia Company House), at the southern tip of Long Beach Island, in 1815. It was followed in 1822 by the Mansion of Health, erected at what was still, in those times, called the Great Swamp, where Surf City is today. The 120-foot structure was about one tenth of a mile from the ocean beach; an ox cart was provided for the convenience of the few lady guests. They enjoyed riding along the surf and visiting the Inman's house nearby, where Aaron's descendants still were able to leave a few whalebones bleaching on the sands.

By at least 1809, stage routes had begun regular, if uncomfortable, service through the Pines. One stage ran from Burlington to Manahawkin, a day's trip, another from Camden to Tuckerton, an overnight journey which was followed on a two-day schedule. Those were the days before Pharo's steamers, so baymen picked up a few cents shuttling passengers across the gap to Long Beach in small sailboats.

Captain Thomas Bond came to the sea beach in 1846 because of failing health. The move was apparently a successful one and, as a bachelor, Bond needed something to occupy his time. On January 30, 1851, he bought the Philadelphia Company House (formerly Horner's) from Lloyd Jones, and renamed it the Long Beach House. It stood facing the bay, about 300-yards from the water.

The fare at Bond's establishment was spartan, with most of the food raised right on the island, even to sheep and other livestock. Bayberry tallow candles were used for illumination, exuding their pungent aroma when extinguished. The tariff however, was enviably low, $1 a day, and between $5 and $7.50 for the week, including room, board, and good fellowship. Bond had an eagle caged on the grounds, which he had caught near the inlet pirating fish from an osprey.[4] It was said that it never got very tame but that Bond was proud of it anyway.

[4]The number of osprey were badly diminished by DDT residues for decades, and are only now recovering population strength.

A characteristic of early resort life was its informality. Some of the early houses had but one room, a curtain running its length to separate the ladies from the gentlemen — at least separation was intended. To the consternation of resort owners, boarders generally turned out to be incurable practical jokers. Bond returned from Tuckerton one day to find one of his cows atop the roof bellowing for aid. Another time, the boys padded the hooves of two mules with burlap and turned them loose, suddenly unmuffled, in a hall of the top floor. They delighted also in rolling wooden bowling balls in the corridors, which echoed through the thin walls like thunder.

Perhaps not incidentally, donkeys and cows were scarce on the island then and were customarily kept under lock and key. The jokers, not to be deterred, hung a mule's-head mask in front of a shawl, draped it over a two-man, improvised quadruped, and tromped raggedly through the halls. An old house, which Lloyd Jones had owned, was sold to Bond to quarter sheep. In later years someone had painted "Y.M.C.A." on one side of it.

A Dip

The beach-goer today may think nothing of several hours in the refreshing billows of our Atlantic, not to mention a good healthy broil beneath a summer sun.[5]

In the 1880s however, things were somewhat different. Sun was, of course, virtually taboo, completely so for women, and bathing, according to writer William Ulyat, was an activity to be indulged with care. Two or three minutes only, and that but a couple of times a week, was his recommendation for ladies, children and delicates. The more robust might bathe daily, but then only for fifteen minutes, at the risk of "exhaustion and chilliness."

Swimming has therapeutic values, he admits, entreating one to take a soapy bath while in the surf. Much cleaner than home, says he, and, upon emerging, a rubdown evokes dreaminess and a desire for sleep. "The reaction sets in favorably..."

On the subject of attire, Ulyat and his contemporaries agree that the commonest, everyday-clothes are appropriate when bathing with family or among friends. More formal mode, however, suggests for both ladies and gentlemen, one piece suits incorporating stunning pantaloons, which sag and drip attractively while wet. A loose covering coat was worn modestly over all. The rage was all for gay colors, flashy grays, brown, or perhaps dark blue flannel. Accessories, in kind, of matching flannel sun hat and dainty sandals, were optional.

It seems, also, that women could be demurely wheeled into the water aboard so-called bathing machines, which doubled as dressing rooms. Imagine a legion of those pink brocaded monstrosities trundling toward the surf!

The average person, however, generally didn't own a suit for bathing, a sport rarely indulged in, and accordingly, rentals were made available in the larger resorts, at a half-dollar a dip. Needless to say, the suits for men and women passed from wearer to wearer many times between cleansings and were thus dull and dirty, often clammy from incomplete drying. Although "more fit for a gutter than a lady's wear," I guess they gave enjoyment. Rare was one so candid, however, as the forward-looking chap who, in 1871 commented: "What a comical looking set of folks we are, attired in our bathing robes."

Above and beyond bathing, then at best a cumbersome affair, the resort guest could ride on the beach or through the dunes, comb the beach for shells, or play at some less active game. The swing was a popular item, especially for the ladies, and they seemed to draw the fellows with them. In those days before the bathing cap was invented, it was considered a great treat to dry the soaking tresses of a pretty maid — the number of lads vying for the privilege was a measure of the girl's popularity.

Fishing, too, held some lure for the resort-goer. Crabbing was an accepted pastime for ladies and children, being carried on in the bay and backwaters, free from the rigors of open ocean. The more hearty sought fairer game at sea, and, towards this end, many enterprising baymen anchored offshore in little sloops and catboats offering a day's fishing trip at four dollars a head. At Toms River, catboats could be chartered for the day for five dollars. Unfortunately, the captains generally were up for charter only when the pound nets and handlines weren't doing too well, which didn't give the part-time fisherman a decent crack at his game.

Author John T. Cunningham writes that some brave souls were casting through the surf about 1881, but others seem fixed on the date of 1907, when a Mr. and Mrs. Charles E. Gerhard were at Long Beach Island. One summer morning, Mrs. G., attired in bathing suit, marched bravely into the breakers with her fishing pole and shortly hauled up a 20-pound channel bass. The possibilities were soon thereafter exploited, and in 1913, a Mr. Holt caught a 56-pound specimen. Since then, of course, the once-esoteric clan of surf fishermen has expanded astronomically. With profuse gear, they trundle to the beach in lavishly equipped "sand bugs," usually a jeep, and fish before dawn day after day.

Meanwhile, Back at the Resort

We have perhaps wandered from our talk about life at Bond's in the old days. Archelaus R. Pharo, our steamship friend from Tuckerton, began offering ferry service to Bond's Long Beach House. He took his wife there, hoping that she would secure relief from her hayfever[6] during that season. She was so improved that Pharo, in partnership with other investors, bought up tracts of beachfront, built another boarding establishment, and started a

[6]At that time, Dr. Herbert A. Willets claimed that "fully eighty-five percent of all cases {of hayfever} are definitely relieved at Long Beach." One must add, however, that the idea, and a valid one, is relief, not a complete cure. A pollen-laden land breeze will set eyes and noses to running again.

village. Thus the Parry House, and Beach Haven, were born. Pharo's daughter ended the search for a name for the new village when she suggested "Beach Haven," while Dr. Willets, a more enthusiastic local resident, had wanted Beach "Heaven."

Bond ran his Long Beach House until 1886, when competition and debt caused its sale to a Charles B. Freeman. The hotel failed in 1888, and was torn down after standing deserted another twenty years.

Fortunately, an old friend, James H. Holgate, gave the impoverished captain (Bond had retired without pension from the life-saving service.) a cottage on the island and supplied him with the necessities. He died, unheralded, at the age of ninety-three.

In the early days, Bond and Pharo were far from alone on the island. In the 1840s Captain Sammy Perrine, of the famous boat-building Perrines, established his famous Harvey Cedars Hotel.[7] He was hotly pursued by John Brown and his four sons, who opened Ashley House up near Barnegat Inlet in 1855.

It was in the last quarter of the 19th century, however, that Long Beach Island felt the first real surge of her growth. Long Beach City came about in 1873, but its name was too easily confused with the whole island and was later changed to Surf City. By 1900, the town had a seething horde of nine souls in permanent residence, and the Great Swamp, filled in by the hurricane of 1821, had disappeared.

Barnegat City reared its young head beneath the light in 1881; Peahala, originally a gun club I believe, followed in 1882. North Beach Haven came along in 1887. The Spray Beach Hotel became the nucleus for the town of Spray Beach in 1890. This area had been known formerly as Cranberry Hill, due to a supposed proliferation of the fruit in that region. Ship Bottom was shoe-horned in at the time of the Spanish American War, in 1898, with only a single house to her name. She did a bit better, however, when the automobile bridge planted its foot on her shore.

The early founders of the Long Beach resorts were either Quakers, such as the Pharo family, or of strong Quaker extraction. It was their desire to maintain a basically sedate atmosphere and, in spite of inevitable jokers, they managed to enforce the mood in a lasting manner. Thus, today the island is still a family resort, with virtually none of the boardwalk honky-tonk that so often creeps in.

[7] *The Harvey Cedars Hotel, now the Harvey Cedars Bible Conference, is the last remaining hotel of its size and vinatge on the Jersey Shore.*

Island Beach

Had there been reason to make a detailed independent map of Island Beach about 1870, it would have been a shockingly barren thing, virtually blank except for a little fishery at Chadwick. Chadwick being a time-honored family name in the vicinity, there came, appropriately, one Elijah Chadwick, who purchased the old Bay Head lifesaving station, which was the first, and then the only, structure in that area. In 1879, it was still the only house, but more were on the way. Chadwick had sold twelve acres at $110 per acre to the borough of Bay Head, a corporation headed by Mr. D. H. Mount, in October of the previous year. Two more houses were erected the following winter and others naturally followed. By 1883 the town had a summer population of about a thousand. Sailing was then as now, one of the main attractions. There was a dock lying at the foot of Chadwick Street where "safe yachts manned by experienced captains could be hired at any time."

Bay Head grew rather quickly, with twenty-two houses being built in 1882 alone. It soon drew a large following amongst the faculty of Princeton University, and many streets today bear the influence of this in their distinguished names.

Perched on the south bank of the Manasquan was a little spot called Sand Town that, in the 1850s, gave up its name for a more commercial Point Pleasant, according to Brick Township historians. Some years later a commercial pavilion sprang up near Manasquan Inlet and a few pleasure boats were moored in a tidal cut. The money began to trickle in and, by 1913, a 900-foot fishing pier was built out from the beach. A storm in 1948 destroyed most of it and the remaining stump was leased to a private source.

The Baptists, taking a cue from the Methodist's success farther up the coast at Ocean Grove, decided to purchase some dune-space on Island Beach. In 1876 they created Seaside Park, a 300-acre respite from the immorality of a secular world. There they meditated in counterpoint to a lonely sea. Contemporary to this effort was Lavallette, named for Admiral Elie La Vallette, first commander of the United States Navy, whose son founded the community. In 1878, Captain John Arnold began barging loads of topsoil across the bay near Swan Point. These, he spread liberally on the dunes, planted some grass, and began selling lots. His ef-

forts became Mantoloking, today an exclusive community characterized by many stately, and a few ostentatious, homes. Seaside
Heights came in 1911, a close parallel to the auto bridge, It was
founded by the Manhasset Realty Company, composed of the five
Cummings brothers.

So it went, product of many motives: religious, medical, economic, and the beaches changed. Where solemn, round dunes
once shouldered alone against the sea, a hundred thousand lights
run a gamut of honky-tonk from one end to the other. Alas, for
the social critic, there remain only a few islands of the primeval
and all too many of the old ways are lost.

We shall omit the morbid tale of the sprawl which followed
World War II. A fungus of housing developments has virtually
encrusted the sea-beaches. They serve, no doubt, the wishes of a
mass population flux to the shore, bringing accommodations there
within reach of those who would otherwise be unable to afford
them. Yet, on the Island Beach peninsula, hundreds of tiny cubes
march in ordered monotony across miles of broiling naked gravel.
There was so little of the beautiful coastline to begin with, why
could it not have been utilized with intelligence and imagination?

Even the silent marshes are being pumped over with shaky footings of sand and mud for development. Such created bay frontage
should be left for two or three years to settle properly, but, in general this is not done. I am told that one such area settled a foot in
1956. If settling is not allowed, structures should at least be erected
on firm matting so settlement can occur at an equal rate. This is
too expensive for many developers, who keep a weather-eye on
competitors' price ranges. Labyrinthine lagoons claw rectangular
channels deep into most such areas, often reaching such complexity that water will not circulate for months at a time. Although
frontage creation has been widespread only since about 1951 prime
areas for development are rapidly being exhausted.

In 1959, the population fluctuations inherent in such a sea-
sonal resort situation border on the fantastic. Long Beach Island
averages between 3,000 and 4,000 persons during the winter
months but population leaps to around 80,000 in July. In addition to this, such influxes as those on the Fourth of July bring an
estimated 100,000 persons to the Island (1955). Unfortunately,
near-slum conditions had arisen in such places as the trailer camp

at Holgate, and tourist camps at Beach Haven. The situation at Seaside Heights, one can appraise for himself.

Middle-class housing predominates, however, and is on the increase, thanks to ease of transportation and the post-war boom which has increased the ability of many to own a second home at the shore. Most of the new construction, done with an eye to a season extending into the late fall, includes insulation and heating. A potential retirement community is eagerly anticipated as a stabilizing influence in the resort industry.

Ocean County today nets about one sixth of the state's travel business. In 1957, this share amounted to over $300 million. Only ten percent of this came from the Lakewood resort area, which is most active between Thanksgiving and Easter. The remaining ninety percent is culled from the fifty-some miles of productive coast.

An Anachronism

And who is profiting, even if only incidentally, from all the activity? None other than the original British Colonial Proprietors of "East Jersey," which was a shareholding group which assumed title to much local land following the sad passing of Mr. Carteret. Naturally, the land, some 4,000-square miles of it, was sold off by the ninety-six proprietors over the years. Things were done rather sloppily in those days: compass bearings have changed, some surveys were merely paced by someone stumbling along at night toward a distant flaming barrel of tar. Some were perhaps never made at all. At any rate, the proprietors wait hungrily, with $80,000 to $100,000 in the bank, and, when title can't be found for a wedge of land here and there they swoop down to claim it quite legally. They meet, and have met, on April 13th of every year since 1688 and will do so, no doubt, as long as a grain of sand changes hands in East Jersey.[8]

[8] The original Proprietors of East Jersey disbanded in 1999. Remaining land was given to the county in which it lay. The records are at the New Jersey Archives in Trenton.

Chapter 12

Ships and Sailing

Through the Inlets

Tiny Tuckerton, in centuries past, held the distinction of being one of the three oldest ports of entry in the United States. One might wonder why some of these little ports managed to develop, with so potential a giant as Philadelphia only a few nautical miles distant. Some have proposed that the Egg Harbor area flourished on the meat of smuggled goods that literally poured in prior to the Revolution. Such articles as rum and molasses, staples of the illicit "triangle trade," had been prohibited by the British and thus could not effectively pass through a closely supervised port like Philadelphia. Even with the long trek through pineland in sheet-top wagons, there was still a profit left in their handling.

Trade north of Manahawkin gravitated primarily to New York by coastal sailing vessel. From Cranberry Inlet, however, several commodities traded not only with Philadelphia, but also the West Indies and even England. Among them were lumber, salt, preserved foodstuffs (fish and game), the products of local shipwrights, and eelgrass for use as mulching, packaging, and mattress stuffing.

Casks (with obvious intent) probably went to the West Indies and there was also apparently a market somewhere for furniture of local red cedar.

The Revolutionary War years found British Commodore Hardy's *Ramilles*, an angry-looking, three-decked, seventy-gun, ship-of-the-line, patrolling the coast to stop trade amongst the coastal ports and New York. When our traditional northeasters rumbled in, the good Commodore was forced to beat his ships out to sea or be driven on the shoals. Naturally, as soon as the gales let up, little coasters would dash out the inlets and scud like hell for New York. Not all of them made it from under Hardy's guns but enough succeeded to keep him mad.

Cruising constantly off the coast, Hardy's provisions naturally dwindled, requiring occasional replenishment that led to forage parties being sent ashore in boats for food and beef. He offered to pay, but people, inflamed as they were, would often refuse any money lest they thus offer aid and comfort to the enemy. Reprisals from more violent patriots no doubt played a part, even among those with less delicate consciences.

Following the Revolution, free thinkers foresaw a great potential in the anticipated shift to free trade but, these proponents were overruled by parties still bitter over the Navigation Acts Britain had imposed, which restricted the colonial import and export of goods other than those England wished. These restrictions temporarily wrecked the immensely profitable triangle trade which also shuttled slaves amongst the West Indies, American ports, and Africa's Gold Coast.

War broke out between the British and French in 1792, giving rise to a phenomenal trade boom in neutral America. Tonnage increased eight-fold in fifteen years, to the incidental detriment of England. With the embargo on British goods and a general non-intercourse between the two nations, British-American relations degenerated into the War of 1812 and trade practically disappeared. The mood along our coast was somewhat different this time and, though the depredations of British warships were still feared, local patriots on the Mullica sold tickets to rooftop seats where the interested could watch privateers in action.

Peace came again in 1815, followed by a three-year boom in trade with staple-hungry Europe. The boom faded and, on the national scene, was supplanted by slow and constant growth, marred only briefly by the panic of 1837.

Until well into the 1850s, Toms River stood as one of the most important commercial centers on the south Jersey coast. This countered a trend started in 1812 by Cranberry Inlet's closing, which brought an end to shipbuilding and voided any practical ocean commerce. Lumber and charcoal subsequently were the mainstay of coastal trade during the period.

The area's sea beaches proved a focal landfall for almost all trade approaching New York and even Philadelphia. Sometimes two hundred ships a day would pass in sight of the shore. In fact, in 1870, the famed clipper ship *Young America* set one of the all-time commercial sailing records (for a loaded ship) in a passage of 83 days from San Fransico to New York, at speeds ranging to 365 nautical miles a day! Proud indeed must her New York builder, W. H. Webb, have been.

But it was not the clipper, not even the square rigger, that dominated coastal commerce. The schooner rig was far and wide a mainstay for Jersey skippers. To understand why, we must explore briefly the wind patterns alongshore. Off New Jersey, and most of New England as well, chances are very good that the sailor will encounter a southerly wind, this being the consequence of thermal convection and Coriolis[1] force. From this we derive the famed expression "down east," since vessels sailing north to New England were consistently sailing before or "down" wind. Similarly, the savvy bay-sailor sails "down" Barnegat to Bay Head, at the northern extremity.

Naturally, ships trading along the north-south coastal routes had not only tailwinds, but, on the return voyage, headwinds as well. For such conditions, the "fore and aft" rig proved the best obtainable since square-riggers could make windward progress at best in shallow, slogging tacks. Such could prove dangerous if they were suddenly headed by a fierce northeaster and driven toward the coastal bars. A schooner, being rigged fore-and-aft could, in general, tack quickly and make good windward progress, gaining either the safety of sea room in a gale or the comfort of a coastal port inaccessible to a deep-draft, ocean-going barque.

The schooner reigned supreme, even into the early years of the 20th century, and countless fine, well-adapted vessels slid down

[1] *Air rising over sun-warmed land pulls cool sea air westward towards the coast. Coriolis force in the northern hemisphere diverts this flow to the right, so the wind flows from south or southeast.*

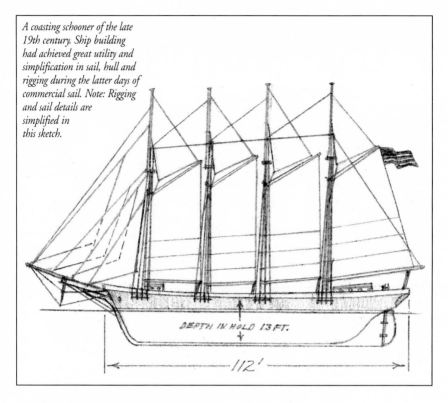

A coasting schooner of the late 19th century. Ship building had achieved great utility and simplification in sail, hull and rigging during the latter days of commercial sail. Note: Rigging and sail details are simplified in this sketch.

DEPTH IN HOLD 13 FT.

112'

the ways to successful careers.

There were however some rather conspicuous failures. The *Thomas W. Lawson* was the largest schooner ever built, her length exceeding 360-feet and her tonnage of 5218 GRT. When she sailed once off Long Beach Island, locals marveled at her seven masts and 25 fore-and-aft sails. To my knowledge, she had more masts than any other sailing vessel built and, without precedent, there was some difficulty naming them. Chroniclers still do not seem in agreement as to how they were tagged but Charles Edgar Nash, of Long Beach Island, remembers that local schoolchildren were taught to recite: "fore, main, mizzen, spanker, jigger, driver, pusher." This behemoth took ten minutes to tack, and, in light weather she was sometimes so hung up in coming about that she had to be pulled round with a yawl. She was at best a hideously cumbersome curiosity and it is perhaps almost as well that she was lost while still a new ship.

Perhaps most impressive about the schooner trade is the vast number of vessels. New Jersey, in comparison with the entire coast,

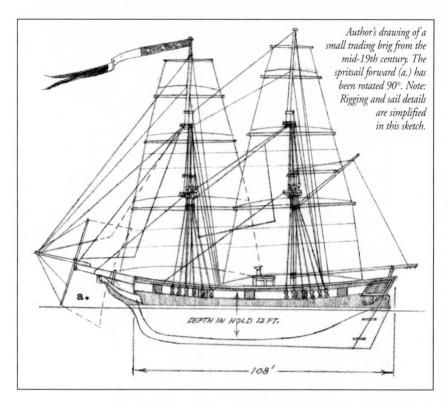

Author's drawing of a small trading brig from the mid-19th century. The spritsail forward (a.) has been rotated 90°. Note: Rigging and sail details are simplified in this sketch.

a.

DEPTH IN HOLD 12 FT.

←——— 108' ———→

handled only a segment of the lumber trade but still, families like the Cavaliers on the Mullica remembered when fifteen or twenty sailing ships anchored daily off Lower Bank. Mr. A.K.H. Doughty told of standing above the Mullica forks and counting 152 ships loaded with wood in the river!

By 1860, U.S. trade had reached an annual total of $700 million despite the fact that exhausted land and increasing costs had obliterated the slave market and, consequently, the triangle trade. Much of the void opened by these events was filled by trade with the emerging South American countries. With the Civil War, schooner values doubled, then tripled. Risks were great, but so intensely needed were supplies that a single cargo would often pay for the ship. War-trade, in fact, was so profitable, that schooner captains from Toms River, Forked River, Waretown, and Barnegat were able to capitalize the Ocean County National Bank in Toms River, and were eventually instrumental in bringing rail service to the area.

World trade felt a turning point in 1860, and, because of privateer action during the Civil War, low profits abroad, and increasing cost, the competition from foreign ships began to decrease. Coasting schooners, with typical American self-interest, were still protected by old laws restricting the coastal trade to U.S. built and owned ships. Between 1860 and World War I, the larger proportion of such bulk goods as coal, iron, lumber, sand, and stone were carried in the coastal trade. In such low profit-margin goods, commercial sail was able — in fact, forced — to linger far beyond its sisters in ocean trade.

Late in the 19th, and into the early 20th centuries mo,re than a score of coasters traded regularly out of Barnegat Bay, first carrying bog iron, then pinewood, and later charcoal, bringing back "store goods" from New York and other cities. Cornelius Larison and his tenting companions arose at 4:30 on a June morning in 1882 and counted along the horizon a steamer, a man o' war, a sloop, three full rigged ships, a bark, and a vessel hull down showing only her masthead.

Still, a rail network of advancing complexity and efficiency, was carrying, by 1914, ten times the goods by weight than coastal traders, and doing it more surely, quickly, and safely — if at a loss, in my opinion — of considerable color. Before we entered World War I , foreign trade again was sparked by the demands of European belligerents. With our own participation the railroads were nationalized and the "slow coaster" began to perish in the wake of new efficiency. At the same time, the Kaiser's *Unterwasserbooten* (submarines) began raising their periscopes and taking toll of their own via torpedoes. A final depletion began in 1914 when many schooners were sailed abroad to satiate a trade and tonnage demand in France during the war. Many were lost and most of the remainder were too old and poor to stand the voyage home.

The latest photograph I know of, contemporary with the sailing coaster off Jersey was taken by a Mr. Neary about 1926. In the distance a badly-hogged old veteran is limping southward with only a single gray shroud of canvas drooping from one of three warped masts. She hardly symbolized the fine pride of old but, I suppose, succeeded in evoking a proper nostalgia for the end of a time-honored trade in sail.

Shipbuilding

Harvey Cedars took its name ultimately from the prolific growth of the Great Swamp that choked the west shore of Long Beach Island centuries ago. Coupled with ample pine forests for pitch and planking, and with bog iron resources for fastenings, colonists found full-measure of the necessities for shipbuilding.

The beginnings are implied before 1700, in the local construction of whaleboats by visiting whalers. According to H.I. Chapelle of the Smithsonian Institution, only one drawing exists of an 18th century pulling-boat of this type, this being a Greenland craft, with pronounced rocker[2] in her keel about 24 feet long. Thanks to longshore whalers, the whaler-type had great popularity in the colonies, developing into a straight keeled craft better suited for surf operations. Size also increased, possibly linked to a greater variety of employment by colonists later than the whalers. They were built of very light cedar so that they could actually be carried by a number of men. Double-enders, they ranged to about 30-feet and had high gunwales permitting them to be loaded deeper than most craft their size.

[2]Ends of the keel, turning up from horizontal, making a boat more maneuverable but less stable while holding a course.

In design, a system was employed known as whole moulding, which dictated that all sectional curves in the craft's hull be determined by systematic shifting of two pre-set templates. By certain extensions of the method, a degree of fineness could be obtained in a vessel's lines but in general a fuller craft resulted than was obtained by later, less rigorous design methods.

Fittings, and even tools that were not imported, came from local forges. The shipwright's primary tool was the adze; a hoe-like axe attached to a handle known as the helve.[3] In the hands of an expert they were effective tools for hewing curved members but are seldom seen anymore.

[3]Late in the 20th century, a broad resurgence of traditional wooden boat building has made these tools available again.

While the whaleboats of colonial days may have been a bit more rotund than their later progeny, there are reports that with a crew of fifteen, they could move at 12-miles per hour under oars alone. And certainly they provided a basis of sorts for the excellent life-saving vessels and Seabright skiffs of the 19th century.

As the colonies matured, sophistication naturally progressed amongst the shipwrights as well. By 1790, yards at Toms River,

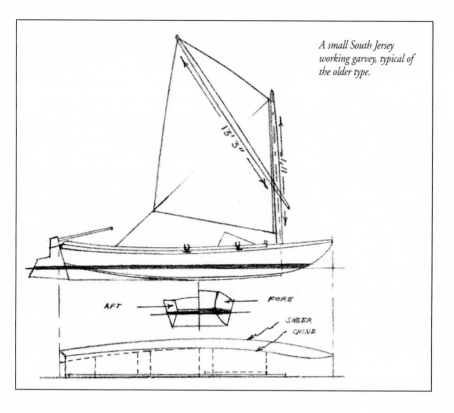

A small South Jersey working garvey, typical of the older type.

Barnegat, Forked River and Tuckerton were building vessels of from five to eight hundred tons burden for the coastal trade. They were customarily rigged as brigs, an illustration of which is found on page 159. As many as five at a time were found building at Tuckerton. The same town, between 1842 and 1867, turned out thirty-nine schooners in sequence. On the knoll at Upper Landing in Barnegat, builders such as Isaac Van Sant, James Morse, Charles Sprague, and others, turned out a fleet that included fifteen schooners and a pair of sloops.

The Leeks began building boats on the Mullica between 1712 and 1715. They continued to do so, turning out, in later years, some of the finest coasting schooners ever built. At the close of the second World War, their shop stood about where our old acquaintance Eric Mullica had his cabin. Charlie Leek, then in charge, was a veteran of the early coastal lifesaving stations, and bore testimony to it by injury in his left eye. The Leek's Works, effectively modernized, today turn out among the finest pleasure craft in the country. It is reputed that the family's name was once Leak but, if so, any concrete evidence of the fact has been thoroughly hidden.

With the advent of an extensive wood-hauling trade on Barnegat Bay, craft were needed that could navigate comfortably in shallow and generally inaccessible, waters to reach the depot where wood was brought from the Pines. The bay craft developed were of shoal nature, probably with centerboards, and about thirty to sixty tons burden, enabling them to carry from twenty-five to fifty cords of wood. Rigged as sloops or schooners, they could be handled easily by a skipper and three paid hands, who received from $8 to $10 a month. Customarily, between December and March, the bay was frozen over, at least much of the time. This kept the bay craft in their slips — and the crew in their taverns. As we discussed previously, these vessels generally confined their trade to the bay, transferring bulk cargoes to other ships for outside hauls.

Jarvis Pharo, it is recorded, came to the colonies aboard the ship *Shields*, upon which we also received the venerable Mr. Leeds, in 1678. Jarvis vegetated along the Delaware before coming to the coast in 1705, where he built a mill on Westecunk Creek.

Local needs dictated much to a boatbuilder in those days and, around the bay area demands included shallow draft, carrying capacity, easy propulsion, and a measure of seaworthiness to overcome Barnegat's perennial southerly chop. Jarvis Pharo, called "Gervas" or "Garvey" by his friends, was still living at Westecunk about 1720 when, it is said, he built a boat that nicely fitted all these criteria. Fittingly, it came to be known as the garvey, a type of craft that has survived, with modifications, to the present. Emerson Farley — whom we quote from the writing of Henry Charlton Beck — defines the garvey as the "oldest Jersey boat." In basic form, the garvey was a flat-bottomed craft, ranging between 18- and 20-feet in length. The topsides angled outward to create what is called "flare." This served to increase stability, load carrying ability, and incidentally, to turn aside small waves that would otherwise slop in. The bottom, at bow and stern, was given "rocker," thus sweeping

Skeeter, a 15-foot Barnegat sneakbox of the later vintage, built by the Perrine family prior to World War II.

upward and out of water — again to turn aside the water, and make her drive more easily. Both bow and stern are square-ended to maximize cargo space. The garvey is generally narrow by other standards, her beam being possibly a quarter or a fifth of overall length. Early garveys were generally rowed or poled and consequently remained small, although Chapelle reports "river garveys" as long as 35-feet. Sail was, of course, soon added to the garvey, usually the common spritsail, with a leeboard or centerboard to reduce side-slip. These craft might well be considered contemporary marine workhorses, as they operated with considerable efficiency in the bay environment as oyster-tonging boats, weir tenders, or for clamming, produce ferrying, and the like.

Chapelle also reports a larger class of sailing garvey, used as oyster dredgers and for general transport. These, he says, were "well-developed sailing scows," mostly gaff-rigged. Since my numerous other sources do not pinpoint the hull type of the bay craft we have discussed in other contexts, they may well have been garveys in the advanced stage. The heavy salt-hay barge (depicted in a previous chapter) by her hull form, may also be considered an extension of the type. It would seem that Jarvis's model went a long way, although Mr. Chapelle seems cautious about giving any small craft an origin so unique.

At least, however, we must uphold the long-continuing nature of the garvey herself, even to a successful transition and modification into the power age. While some of the aesthetic character was often lost, the garvey served well under power when her bottom was straightened out aft (the rocker removed), to prevent squatting at higher, mechanically-induced speeds.

At this point we enter upon a consideration of what is probably New Jersey's best known small boat type. The tale runs back to the early 1830s when gunners on Barnegat Bay used a so-called "sink-box" in their professional hunting trade. This was merely a watertight box, anchored by stakes run through eyes at the corners or through holes in a partial deck that carried beyond the sides. Sunk low in the water with sand or other ballast, they were camouflaged with marsh grass and thus the hunter would await an unsuspecting flock with his huge punt-gun.

In 1836, a boatbuilder and hunter, Captain Hazelton Seaman of West Creek, built a low-decked boat, or gunning punt, which he chose to call "the Devil's coffin." It was designed to fill the concealment needs of the hunter as well as to provide smooth transport to and from the marshes, even against the wind-blown chop that caused the garveys to pound uncomfortably. Baymen, appreciative of her virtues, dubbed her the "sneak-box." The Barnegat sneakbox has been aptly compared to a teaspoon and a melonseed, which quite adequately describes her hull-form. Sneakboxes were, from the first, decked-over, except for a small rectangular cockpit, and early versions rarely went beyond 12-feet. Very shoal boats, they were often fitted with iron-shod wooden runners on the bottom, so that they could be pulled up on the bay-ice with long sharp boat hooks and poled to open water again. The type caught on very quickly and, although builders were often separated by many miles, the type long retained its integrity. Southern Barnegat Bay boats generally had rudders, while those toward Bay Head used an oar at the lee rail to steer. Since they were invariably decked-over, freeboard[4] remained at about 7-inches. When sail entered the picture, a daggerboard[5] (either offset, or somewhat forward, beneath the deck) was installed, and a simple spritsail rigged to an unstayed mast. The spars were short and easily unshipped, almost always being designed to stow inside the boat. With a tight-fitting hatch secured over the cockpit, this made a neat package; quite impervious to the weather and resistant, at least to the casual thief.

Following its general acceptance on the bay, designing and building sneakboxes became the stock-in-trade of the Perrine family of Barnegat, on the mainland. They did their job well, for, in 1928, there was at least one sneakbox that had survived eighty-five years use. As the sneakbox sailing rig developed into a tall and graceful gaff-cat, it became less suited for the hull type than the simple rig of old, especially in over pressing the boats downwind, literally "submarining" them by pushing the spoon shaped bow downward until it plowed under a wave. Edwin Schoettle, a well-known author of sailing and boating books, maintains if a sailor can get "results" from the sneakbox, he can consider himself "well qualified to get something from any small sailboat in existence." A couple of noteworthy voyages have been made in sneakboxes, which attest more to the seamanship and endurance of the skippers than to innate qualities of the boat. In the 1920s, one was made by

[4] *The distance between the level of the water and the upper surface of deck.*

[5] *A removable board on a small sailboat, lowered into the water through a watertight box or trunk to reduce side-slip sailing to windward.*

Slade Dale, from New York to Miami, better than 2,000 miles in a 12-foot model. Nathaniel H. Bishop spent four months in a sneakbox, writing a book about it afterward. His boat, *The Centennial Republic*, was built in Manahawkin.

[6]*Third-generation Beatons are still boatbuilders in the original yard at the time of this writing.*

The sneakbox, as it developed, is credited with being a pioneer in the overhanging bow, at least as it relates to shoal, light displacement hulls. It is reported that the great Herreshoff designed his first boat with an overhanging bow after watching a Barnegat sneak in action. C. Howard Perrine was the last of his family to carry on the type, as it had metamorphosed in recent years. He died in June, 1956, and the still-considerable demand for well-constructed craft was ably assumed by another small-boat patriarch, David Beaton[6] of Mantoloking.

The Amazing Mr. Francis

Perhaps the most prolific contributor to innovative boatbuilding in the Barnegat area was Joseph Francis. He was building his first boats in 1811, just a year before Cranberry Inlet closed, but his influence, and often duplicated ideas, will be with the marine world for centuries to come. In his latter years, Francis lived at the very edge of Toms River, in an imposing home which became the Riverview Hotel in the early 1900s (today it is the site of a condominium development).

As a renowned builder, he constructed a racing skiff for the Czar of Russia that became the first American racing craft to compete with those of a foreign power. Fascinated by time-tested craft from Europe, he built the first Venetian gondola in the United States. He was an early experimenter in molded boats, just recently becoming so popular. He worked with double bottoms, and constructed a perfectly round sailing yacht, named (appropriately or otherwise) the *Sarah Francis*, which was designed to go across the surface of, rather than through, the water. He built the craft in four months, deaf to the jeers of hecklers, who anticipating another generation, called it "flying saucer!" Although the concept proved successful in trials at Toms River, Mr. Francis seemed content to have proved his point and dropped the idea.

Without a doubt, Francis' greatest contribution was his championship of the lifeboat. To be sure, most vessels of the day carried a small boat aboard. It was for use in port, rather than as a lifesaving device. At sea, it was lashed heavily, and inaccessibly, upside down in the "waist" of the ship, by and large the most hazardous spot on a foundering craft. His invention, the Francis Lifecar, in conjunction with the Newell apparatus for passing a line to distressed vessels, was first used to rescue men from the *Ayreshire* shipwreck. For the lifecar and its considerable contribution to the cause of human mercy, Francis was awarded the most massive gold medal ever given by Congress to an individual.

Francis conceived, designed, and later manufactured the lifecar. Basically, it was a small boat of corrugated iron, sealed over with a high-crowned deck and opened only by a tight hatch, through which the passenger(s) would enter. It was designed to run, by block and tackle, along a heavy hawser stretched from the beach to the distressed vessel. The bullet-shape made hauling the car in and out both easier and safer, and, if the cable should break, the occupants would still have a good chance of being driven safely ashore in a tightly sealed capsule.

The first lifecar was constructed in 1843, and subsequent models were produced in a large four-cylinder hydraulic press, which formed each of the craft's sides in a single operation. They proved an invaluable tool as the lifesaving stations began developing their network along the coasts toward mid-century.

The Growth of Pleasure Boating

Some authorities trace yachting in America back as far as Adrian Block's little *Onrest* in 1614, but this would be stretching the point. Would the average boatman today consider his forage into Barnegat Bay, then totally unexplored, a typical weekend cruise?

It is more logical to skip this, and any intervening hypotheses and consider, as a starting point, the 1880s, when men of the lifesaving service began racing sneakboxes for relaxation (and not, incidentally, cash prizes) at the instigation of Henry J. West, a bayside dweller at Seaside Park. With the near-explosive growth of the resort industry, it is hardly surprising that young men visiting the Barnegat area absorbed sailing into their activities. What can compare with the clean thrill, the unique sense of interaction with nature that accompanies the adept helmsman talking his ship to windward?

By 1900, the utilitarian lug-rigged[7] sneakboxes of Seaman and Perrine had metamorphosed into a class of 20-foot racing machines carrying a squat, overpowering sloop, or cat, rig. In the interests of remaining upright in the stiff southerly that frequents the region so many summer afternoons, each boat carried a crew of eight men stacked on the weather rail amongst some thirty-five rope-handled sandbags, each weighing thirty pounds. At each tack, that meant eight bodies and 1,050 pounds of ballast had to shift sides. Ten or twelve seconds coming through stays was considered good time.

[7] Rigged with a lug sail; a quadrilateral sail bent upon a yard that crossed the mast obliquely.

Conditions like the above were unrealistic stages in the development of a truly useful sailboat that could blend a degree of pleasure (e.g., comfort) with speed, and eventually a class for 15-foot sneakboxes came into existence. In 1910, there were fifty of the twenty-foot sandbaggers, but this figure was almost immediately surpassed by the 15-footers, which attained wide and rapid acceptance after their introduction in 1918. They were admitted as a class by the Barnegat Bay Yacht Racing Association in 1922. By and large, the boats have persisted unchanged in large numbers to date. Carrying a rather large gaff-rig, the sailor finds them relatively fleet under mild conditions, although they retain a characteristic tendency to submerge when running under full sail before a breeze exceeding, say, ten or fifteen knots.

Of course the sneakbox, as time passed, was only one breed among dozens that sailed the bay, from ice-boats in the winter months to the big old twenty-eight foot catboats in summer. Few of the big cats remain today, but most of those still sailing race each year in a regatta for the famous Toms River Challenge Cup, billed by *Yachting* magazine as the second oldest active racing trophy in America. The catboat *Mary Ann* won the cup in 1959.[8]

[8] The "A" Cats experienced a rebirth in the late 20th century.

As a type, the cats evolved from basically commercial craft built in the early 1900s. Most of these forebears, having outlived their usefulness as sailing vessels, were converted to power with the passing years. An old photo shows seven such conversions nosed into a pier at Beach Haven Yacht Club, and one, built in the 1880s, was described, in 1936, as still going strong and "a damn good tugboat," although her bottom was so soft that it bent on striking a sandbar. In 1963, an ancient hulk, formerly the *Starfire*, was still afloat at Mantoloking, an ungainly conversion that served as happy summer refuge for a local family.

Boatyards, as such, appear to have begun in 1878, when Benjamin Hance opened his small establishment at Bay Head. He was followed, in 1891, by Mr. Morton Johnson, and in 1912 by Morton's son Hubert, whose yard today builds one of the finest Jersey sea skiffs available. Both Johnson yards[9] still function today alongside one another with relative amicability, and are strangely supplemented by Johnson Brothers, an unrelated firm, all three within a stone's throw of the Bay Head-Manasquan Canal.

[9] These yards have since closed and been largely replaced with residential housing.

In 1955, there were approximately thirty-three boatyards in Ocean County, but, under the impetus of a 4,000 percent increase in the number of small boat owners, this number increased at the beginning of the 1960s to 161 yards and liveries. It is superfluous to point out, even to the casual tourist driving through the area, what scope the marina and boating industry has assumed. Along the New Jersey coast there were, in 1957, some five to six thousand rowboats distributed amongst a hundred liveries. Forty-six of these liveries, and some two thousand boats, were, in 1956, at Long Beach Island alone, with the same narrow strip of sand listing nearly another thousand pleasure and commercial craft. The Barnegat Bay area, as a whole, is believed to have the second largest fleet of pleasure boats in the nation.

The Intercoastal Waterway

A charter was granted by the legislature in 1835, for the excavation of a canal between Manasquan and Bay Head but the project lay fallow through lack of need until about 1908, when the state began preliminary activities. In 1915, partially under the threat of submarine warfare, the federal government opened the Intercoastal Waterway, which allowed craft drawing under 6-feet of water to travel from Lake Erie to Florida with only minimal passage through open water. The Bay Head-Manasquan Canal[10] remained a missing link which forced outside passage between Manasquan and treacherous Barnegat Inlet, which was difficult to enter even in fine weather. After some eight years of on and off digging, the canal, with suitable depth throughout, was opened in 1928. Unfortunately, at least for boats not adequately powered, the canal

[10] The canal, still daunting to modestly-powered boats, was much improved when bridges were rebuilt following the collapse of the Lovelandtown Bridge during the March storm of 1962.

proves almost as fearful as Barnegat Inlet, due to the tidal lag that makes high-water in the upper bay about five hours behind that at Manasquan Jetty, and vice-versa. Currents, according to a local state navigation man, have been clocked at nearly 13-miles per hour, as the bay and river attempt to equalize the disparity.

But notwithstanding such an obstacle, and it is truly a harrowing trip on the full ebb or flow of a tide, Manasquan inlet handles a vast amount of water traffic. John T. Cunningham wrote in 1958 that on a Sunday morning, up to 1,600 boats pass out the inlet leaving the sport-fisherman port of Brielle, and pour up from numerous havens south of the canal. Each year the number increases, apparently without cease. Boating will no doubt continue to provide a significant proportion of sustenance for the Barnegat area. Perhaps, owing to the complexity of the economic organism with which it is enmeshed, boating is more significant than it could ever have been in the past; even when it brought guns for the Revolution or food for survival.

Chapter 13

Wrecks, Lights, And Pirates

The Sea Breaketh

Thirteen is an oddly prophetic chapter numeral under which to discuss a colorful though tragic history. Why should the shore off Barnegat, a straight coastline with relatively regular sand bottom, have proved, over the centuries, such a graveyard of ships? Back once more to Robert Juet, September 2, 1609:

> The mouth of that Lake hath many shoals, and the sea breaketh upon them as it is cast out of the mouth of it.

Indeed, there were many shoals, both at the inlet and for miles up and down the coast. These comprise what coastal geologists consider a submerged system of runnels and bars; which is to say that, parallel to the beach, run longitudinal sandbars, thrown up by the cyclic action of the sea. Usually, these are two in number and separated from the actual shore, and from each other, by a "runnel" or channel of deeper water.

Ships, of course, knew the bars were there andwere generally forced to run along the coast at least a little way after making a landfall, in order to reach New York or Philadelphia. There was also considerable traffic in purely coastal trade both between major ports and amongst the more local inlets.

Storms in this hemisphere are invariably cyclonic, that is the winds in them converge while rotating counterclockwise and spiraling inward around a low pressure center.[1] Such a disturbance, moving along off our coast, will therefore create a northeast wind blowing inshore against the beaches. With a fetch[2] equivalent to the distance of the storm offshore, vast seas invariably develop and crash with relentless fury on the bars. At high water they will sometimes break directly on the beach, sweeping sometimes completely over the sea islands and occasionally carving new inlets, as we have seen. Low water usually brings the "outer" bar close enough to the surface that the surf will break on it, rolling thenceforth across the inner bar and to the beach, a confused tumble of foam.

To the skipper of a ship offshore, the northeast wind meant that, unless he could beat to windward, he would be driven ashore. If the storm were severe enough, his ship might not be able to make way against it, or might even have to run before the wind or risk foundering beneath a series of overwhelming waves. In such straits, if anchors failed to hold, even the most competent captains were forced to ride their ships to death on the bars. In the dark of night, with wind shrieking in the rigging and squalls drowning out the boom of breaking surf, a ship would often crush her bow on the outer bar and swing slowly broadside so the rollers smashed at her sides. Planking would be stove in and the hatches breached. Filling with sand and water, she would roll over and die in the breakers, scattering her cargo and the bodies of her crew for miles along the coast.

Occasionally, a ship would try to hold herself some distance at sea with her anchors. Some succeeded; some didn't.

[1] High pressure, fair weather systems rotate opposite, or clockwise.

[2] The distance over which wave height has the opportunity to increase.

Wreck on the Beach

Perhaps those Roman coins of unknown origin, with which we opened this book many chapters ago, were remnants of the first wreck broken on those shoals, but this we will never conclusively establish. There is an early record of a ship, the *Beaverbrook,* run ashore in October 1684, and Burlington courthouse records indicate the prosecution of men apprehended stealing cargo from her. A considerably more nebulous record comes down on another late 17th century wreck near Egg Harbor, after which a Portuguese sailor, purportedly descended from Vasco DaGama, made his way finally to New York.

Rarely, Spanish coins turn up perched atop little pillars of sand, compressed beneath their weight after storm winds have driven the surrounding layer away. A repeated rumor states that up to five hundred coins, dating from 1682 to 1795, had been found in a single day along Long Beach Island! The silver Spanish milled dollar, or *reale*, was virtually a world exchange standard during the colonial period. The Continental dollar, a paper currency printed by the new United States government, was roughly equivalent to the Spanish dollar and bore the legend:

> This bill entitles the Bearer to receive (   ) Spanish Milled Dollars, or the value thereof in Gold or Silver, according to a Resolution passed by the Congress at Philadelphia September 26th, 1778.

The fabled "piece of eight" literally represented a value equal to eight of the smaller *reales*, and was itself sometimes literally divided into smaller "pieces" when lesser coinage was unavailable. Spanish coinage was also the genesis of our dollar sign ($) from the *reale* sign (8). Other coins, found only on rare occasions, are doubloons and double-doubloons or *onzas*, struck from gold and represented, at the time, respectively, of $12 and $25. Most of the coins recovered are so encrusted that only their shape remains. Immersion in vinegar for from a few days to a month restores much of the original detail, however. Occurrence of Spanish coinage like this, it is well to note, becomes more understandable when we recognize that it comprised the chief exchange medium in the United States through the latter half of the 18th century and remained legal tender here until 1857.

Returning to more mundane matters, we find apparently the first printed record of a wreck on Barnegat shoals in the *Boston News Letter* of May, 1705, citing a New York dateline of April 30:

> Yesterday came hither the masters of three sloops which were cast away near Barnegat by the late Easterly Storms, Viz: *Archibald Morris*, who was bound from Pennsylvania for New York and Boston: one *Jones* who was bound from Horekill[3] to Boston, and

[3] *On the Delaware River.*

one *Saunders* had one man drowned and saved nothing at all, and the others saved very little besides lives.

All too many had not even that good fortune. Again, how many ships went down we will likely never know, but a government chart, carefully cloistered in Washington, locates between 2,100 and 2,200 wrecks off the Jersey coast.

A few more spotty records come down from the earlier years, such as the ship foundering off Cranberry Inlet in October of 1775, which gave up several cannon, sixty muskets and a half barrel of powder before the surf broke her up and the crew was forced to desert her. There was, in addition, a British transport, the *Mermaid*, which came ashore at Egg Harbor in 1779. And another strange revelation: where the "new inlet" cut through slender Island Beach in 1935, a worn wooden case was found in late July or early August of 1936. Its corners rounded severely by sand and sea action, it contained a sextant made after the early fashion and marked with an inscription as follows, in raised lettering:

Made by Edward Gilbert, Tower Hill, London for Will Tillock
April 28, 1778 and etched beneath this, testimony to a change in
ownership:

Z. Wetzell, 1782

What misadventure befell the vessel this instrument had guided, and the supposedly competent hand of "Z. Wetzell," shall ever be an enigma, like as not.

With the 19th century, coastwise and long-distance trade became more prevalent than during the colonial period. Consequently, when writer Harold Watson visited the barrier beaches in 1833, he found them already littered with the bleaching bones of many a once-proud ship. An official report to the congress in 1848 cites 158 vessels which were wrecked in the ten years prior to that date (1839-1848) along the Jersey shore, most of them going up on Long Beach Island and what was then still Squan Beach.

On February 14, 1846, a fierce blizzard reduced visibility on the sea-beaches to a few yards and locals huddled gratefully about their hearths while shutters clattered angrily from the gale. Just off Seaside Park, the full-rigged packet ship *John Minturn* struck the outer bar and hung there with the combers raking her decks mercilessly. A few helpless watchers on the beach caught only a fleeting glimpse of her through the driving snow, enough to perceive her passengers and crew huddled pitifully in the lee of battered deck houses. Drenched with seawater and plastered with snow, they soon froze and, one by one, were swept overboard to their deaths. Of fifty-one souls aboard, forty-two bodies were picked off the beach the next morning and sorrowfully conveyed in an old boat to Bay Head where they were interred in a common grave which may still be seen in a west Point Pleasant cemetery. In what later became known as the "*Minturn* Storm," nine other ships went ashore between there and Sandy Hook.

In April of 1854, the clipper *Powhattan* was approaching New York having left Le Havre with some 340 persons aboard, most of them German immigrants coming to the New World. Off our coast she was struck by a violent northeaster. Her sails all carried away, she drifted, virtually unmaneuverable, and grounded heavily on the shoal 6 miles south of the Harvey Cedars Life Saving Station during the night of April 17. Dozens of persons perished before daybreak, plucked from the rigging by cold and wave. All day, helpless observers on shore, unable to get out a boat through the surf, watched horrified as more succumbed. At about 5 P.M., the sea had apparently played long enough and sent a huge comber to sweep every remaining soul from the wreck. What sick, blood curdling cries must have been heard as the balance of the three hundred and forty lives were sucked out by that boiling wave. Bodies were strewn for 25-miles along the coast. Although the *Powhattan* disaster was the worst our coast has ever seen, she was, unfortunately, not alone on the sacrificial altar of that terrible day. Fate had seen fit to cast up the schooner *Manhattan*, out of Bangor, Maine, with the loss of ninety lives aboard her.

Ten years later, in 1864, one brutal week saw the loss of six major vessels on Long Beach Island alone. During a 40-year period, from 1838 to 1878, more than 125 ships were lost between Barnegat Inlet and Sandy Hook, an average of better than five ships per mile. For every year between 1878 and 1889, a ship went down off Bay Head, four of them being lost in exactly the same spot.

In later years, with the increasing efforts of the lifesavin g service, ships offshore had better luck, and the advent of steam power was also instrumental in giving the skipper better control over his ship in heavy weather. Still, ships continued to be sacrificed. In addition to almost countless lumber and trading schooners, there was the famed clipper ship, *Andrew Jackson,* which came up on Long Beach shoals. She held the record for a sailing ship passage between New York and San Francisco of eighty days around Cape Horn. And there was the Austrian barque, *Kraljevica,* which struck the bar at 1:30 A.M. on February 10, 1886. She had sailed from Fiume, Italy, with a cargo of salt. Her crew fired a flare for assistance from the beach but were soon forced to abandon their bilged ship. Captain Sverljuga and his crew of thirteen took to their longboat and ranged through heavy seas parallel to the coast until there appeared a break in the surf sufficient for them to land near the Ship Bottom Life Saving Station. At daybreak, they attempted to run in, but the boat broached-to and capsized. Eight of its occupants drowned and the balance, nearly frozen, managed to creep to a gunner's box (duck blind) in the dunes, where they found some provisions and rudimentary heat and clothing.

As fate would have it, the lifesaving service men on Long Beach had seen the flare sent up from the *Kraljevica,* and, after a two hour struggle in the surf, managed to get their boat out to her. Finding the barque deserted, they attempted to reach the beach again but, their boat, being heavy with water taken over the gunwales, was swamped by a comber 400-yards offshore, and of the seven men aboard only four survived, two of them found unconscious. One, a member of the Inman clan, never really recovered from the shock of this experience and soon "went blind" from exposure and died without ever going to sea again. Marble shafts were erected over the graves of the three dead men and a pension was established for their families by the Austrian government. Better luck awaited the crew of the Italian barque *Fortuna,* which grounded one night during the winter of 1909-1910. All aboard were saved, including a newborn baby, a pig, and the ship's cat.

Even the steamer was not immune to those deadly shoals. There was the *Idaho* as early as 1865, the *Starlight* on October 6, 1875, and, on November 19, 1884, the 330-foot red-hulled *Guadeloupe.* The *U.S.S. Culgoa* succumbed on November 9, 1901, and on Long Beach Island, December 11, 1916, the U.S. troopship *Sumner,* bound for the Panama Canal, ironically broke up on a pile of her own cargo jettisoned by the crew to lighten and float her. All 299 aboard were saved, but the hull cracked in two and collapsed in a week.

Returning to sail, which during the progression of dates outlined above had virtually died out as a commercial entity, we find the unfortunate *J. Holmes*, a lumber schooner, lost ashore in September 1917. The most recent record I have of a commercial sailing vessel wrecked on this coast is the *Cecil P. Stewart* at Harvey Cedars in 1927.

In April 1963, a friend and I found an olive-drab, enameled metal flask amongst the dunes on Island Beach, rusted through in several spots but with a disk near the neck reading: *Osterreich Fabrik* (Made in Austria), 1918 . We hypothesized that it dated from very early submarine incursions off our coast during World War I. With the advent of World War II, German submarines created a serious menace, and at least ten ships were torpedoed in sight of land off the Jersey shore. Many a day our beach was strewn with congealed oil and an occasional life-jacket. During the 1940s, German U-boats came as close as a mile to our beach. And, during that conflict, two of our own destroyer escorts managed to blunder onto the shoals in a fog one night. This spoke ill, I suppose, of their ability to locate a sub, since they had trouble anticipating the bottom off their own shores.

During subsequent years, a number of ships approached too close to the shoals and ran aground. Construction had, however, improved to the point where the contemporary ship could often withstand the resultant strains on her hull. My first visit to Barnegat Light, about 1952, presented me with the sight, one April afternoon, of a freighter aground within a mile of the lighthouse. She was floated in about two days. And in the midst of the "Great Atlantic Storm" of March 1962, the moth-balled destroyer *U.S.S. Monssen* broke loose from the tug towing her. While Long Beach Island was inundated by breaking seas, the *Monssen* washed up on the beach a scant 300-feet from where I had parked my car a few weeks before. A young Navy captain was killed by a breaking steel cable during efforts over the next month to free her. The incident was virtually duplicated in early March 1963, when a likewise moth-balled minesweeper dragged her tug ashore right on the beach at Harvey Cedars. The extraction of both was finally effected at great expense.

Mortality

It is apparent from the record that in later years, fatalities during wrecks thankfully became the exception rather than the rule. However, during the late 18th and most of the 19th centuries, death was a co-habitor of the beaches. It was estimated by one writer that between four-and five-hundred human lives were lost on these shoals. In one chapter alone, you can total 640.

Barring special cases such as the *Minturn*, victims were customarily carried behind the dunes and interred in shallow graves with a minimum of ceremony. All too often, by the time a corpse was recovered, it was in a bloated or decayed condition and could not be held for identification. My uncle told us of a young man who had drowned along the Jersey shore earlier in this century. He was dragged from the surf with a rope up to the beach, bloated and stinking, while the crabs dropped reluctantly from his flesh and crept back to the sea.

On occasion, we are told, storms shifting beach sands will uncover "old unmarked graves, revealing grisly reminders of the sea's voracity." Rumor has it there are some fifteen graves at Barnegat Light, and possibly three on Island Beach. Some bodies, of course, found their way to local cemeteries where those were available, but it was not until 1904 that the state established the policy of erecting monuments for them. A few of those set up were at Whitelawn Cemetery in Point Pleasant, Riverside Cemetery in Toms River, and the Baptist churchyard in Manahawkin. The initial monument was at Point Pleasant, where three granite spires were erected in 1904 bearing the legend: "The Unknown from the Sea."

The plot was maintained originally by the Bureau of Navigation, but since 1955, this duty has been ceded to the Department of Conservation and Economic Development.

Clarence F. Lee, a trustee of the Whitelawn Cemetery, recalled in 1959 that the last shipwreck corpse had been interred there around 1929, when he helped his grandfather open the grave. A survey, it is said, may someday be attempted to determine the identity of those buried in what amounts to a mass grave but, "this will take time" officials maintain. Any evidence still lingering could likely be lost by then, and the anonymous dead will so remain.

Metamorphosis

Over the centuries, wrecks, in and of themselves, worked a strange metamorphosis on the Barnegat area and their influence, indeed, extended into some of the most surprising places. In 1817, a storm raged up the coast and in the midst of it, legend tells us, Captain Stephen Willets of Tuckerton felt a strange urge to go to sea. He set sail up the coast and, purely on a hunch, sent his crew ashore around present-day Ship Bottom, where they discovered a ship in the shoals, bottom up. Hearing tapping from the hull, they found a woman inside. She thanked her rescuers in a foreign tongue, either Spanish or Italian, and when they brought her ashore to recover, she immediately knelt in the sand and drew a cross. There is no record of her, or the ship's, name. In 1947, the town formally took the name "Ship Bottom" in commemoration of that strange event 130 years before.

During another storm, on September 10, 1846, the sloop *Adelaide* was making a run for Barnegat Inlet, with Captain James Lamson from Cedar Run at her helm. When she struck a bar and capsized, all hands, it appeared, must have perished. Two Barnegat Inlet locals, Charles Collins and Garret Herring, found the hull on the beach. To their amazement, from within they heard faint tappings, barely audible through the storm's din. Upon breaking laboriously through the planking of the hull, they were totally dumbfounded to find a young girl pinned by a cabin partition and hanging with her head just above the water. It was Captain Lamson's daughter, Edith. Locals state that, until her death in 1926, she regularly visited the beach near where she was rescued, and where her father and three crewmen, all Barnegat natives, met their deaths.

Animal life too, felt the influence of wrecks. A local tale says that, during the Revolution, "Uncle" Caleb Parker, later the faithful keeper of Barnegat Light, and known by those frequenting Bond's resort as the "Barnegat Pirate," rescued a cat from a British ship that went ashore near Barnegat Inlet. It had no tail, and disproportionately short front legs that caused it to walk with a strange hopping gait. In a few days she gave birth to a litter. There were reports in 1914 that some descendants of the British cat still remained in the area.

There is a similar tale centering about Bay Head where, in 1869, a ship came ashore and went to pieces on the bar. At some point in her wanderings she had numbered amongst her crew two cats of a tailless breed from the Isle of Man, and these two Manx cats came ashore to spread their kind far and wide. This story has rather strong evidence, for in the last ten years, I have seen the old Manx gene crop up a few times in tailless kittens around local boatyards between Bay Head and Mantoloking.

In the late 1880s the brig *Antioch,* bearing a cargo variously labeled as iron ore and marble, foundered off Manasquan Inlet in a gale. With her heavy cargo intact, she settled straight to the bottom, her masts protruding to the topgallant crosstrees.

In 1879, the government had spent $39,000 — then a tidy sum — to erect beach-stabilizing jetties north of Manasquan Inlet. In 1889 Gustav Kobbe wrote that the wreck of a Spanish brig (this may have been the *Antioch*) had so disturbed the littoral current flow that, despite the jetties, the inlet had nearly closed.

In 1908, the federal government began excavating for the Bay Head-Manasquan Canal that was opened to tidal flow in 1925. Local philosophers maintain the canal "drained the flow" from Manasquan Inlet, allowing the passage to close completely in 1926. In August of that year, fire hoses and the strong backs of National Guardsman re-opened the passage, but, between 1928 and 1929, it closed again with a 10-foot sand barrier of drifting dunes. Water stagnation and dying marine life brought concerted action on a federal, state and municipal level and a 400-foot channel bordered by two rock jetties was begun in 1930. On February 10, 1931, ocean and river met with the full moon tide. The May, 1933 *National Geographic Magazine* reported that in spite of the jetties, a new sand barrier "wider than the beach" was thrown up. This was later dredged out, and, it is reported by other sources, the *Antioch* was dynamited around 1938, to reduce her to the point where she could no longer be a menace to navigation. Just what her effect was on the geography of Manasquan Inlet remains a point of conjecture but, nevertheless, an interesting one.[4]

Over the years, shipwrecks cast their various cargoes onto New Jersey's shores. The *Imperatrice Elizabetta* met her fate on Long Beach in 1868 and, as she broke up, cases of cargo began floating ashore into the eager arms of local salvagers. Anticipating a rich "harvest of the sea," they broke open case after case. It is said that

[4]*Decades after* Closed Sea *was written, Manasquan attorney John Wooley dug out an old photograph in which horses with sand scoops were encouraging currents to scour through the newly re-opened Manasquan Inlet channel. In the foreground, by chance, stand two young people, Stan and Pauline Mountford, the author's then-youthful father and aunt!*

for years thereafter prunes (for there was nothing but prunes) appeared on the Island menus in multitudinous form.

[5] A class of mostly ship-rigged vessels trading to the Pacific around Cape Horn, at South America's stormy tip.

The twenty-five man crew of the Cape-Horner[5] *Francis* made good the bulk of their passage from California until, off the Atlantic coast, their ship took fire and they led her cautiously along shore. Apparently unable to extinguish the flames, the crew tried to manage them lest they get out of control. It was their object to be near the beach if their lives were put in jeopardy. On May 1, 1897, she went aground on the bar off Little Egg Harbor Inlet and, later, the fire took on such proportions that a Long Beach Island lifesaving crew came out to get her men. Shortly thereafter the extensive cargo of salmon and wine aboard *Francis* began coming ashore. It was soon distributed amongst woodshed and attic about the Island.

The ship's owners engaged a salvage company to re-acquire what they could of the property, to which end they offered locals $3 per barrel. They managed to secure some three thousand kegs in the process, but I'll wager they got more salmon than wine for, it is said, Long Beach was a mighty tight little island for a long time.

The *Francis* booty flowed smoothly into the regional culture and was seemingly distributed amongst Methodist, Presbyterian, Quaker and "freethinker" without regard to prevailing views on temperance. Nine varieties of spirits reportedly came out of the ship. Two young ladies, previously strangers to the vice, lost track of the brands they had sampled long before their totally scandalized mothers could roll them into bed.

Historian Henry Charlton Beck reports an interview with "Chink" Simpkins about the liquor:

> ..but it wasn't nothin compared with what we got aholt of when the Good Ship *Francis* was wrecked. Why, once you let that stuff trickle down, it was a full two minutes before you got your breath. The liquor of the *Francis* was strychnine, that's what it was.

It is said that as late as 1914 you could get a little glass of *Francis* brandy, but to do so required a great amount of tact with the few jealous locals who guarded the remnants of that happy accident.

Barnegat Pirates

The wrecks had influenced diet and, perhaps, morality on the beaches. But note a common thread: locals felt perfectly justified in claiming the cargo of any ship which ill-met their shore. That right is almost legendary and is the basis of the present segment of our tale.

The course of William Kidd, as it is generally known to the public in its sordid form, began on December 11, 1695, when he was commissioned as a privateer by the British Crown. He sailed in the English ship *Adventure* whose mission it was to rid the sea of pirates. Off Madagascar, the *Adventure* met a Moorish merchant-man, the *Squede Marchan,* which she was to escort. Conveniently, Kidd chose that moment to turn pirate himself and, capturing the *Squede*, he purportedly sailed her to Hispanola and sold her, buying with the proceeds a less notorious American-built sloop, the *San Antonio*. Legend has it that Kidd and his crew, heading north along the Atlantic seaboard of the Americas, lay in along many obscure beaches and secreted segments of the rich booty he had acquired. Two spots are mentioned in such connection in the Barnegat area.

Kidd was finally apprehended with ten of his men and tried for his crimes. In May of 1701 he was led from his trial at old Bailey in London to a gibbet near Tiburn Fort. There, his body tarred and triced up in chains, he was hung. It is said that in dying he confessed fully the error of his ways, but, of course, it is apparent that he revealed nothing about where his booty was hidden.

History records that at least three of the men tried with William Kidd were acquitted and it is further reported that one "definitely" was known to have settled, under the name of Bennet, one mile south of Barnegat on a Manahawkin road. It is thus, goes the tale, that the place was called Bennet's Neck.

Another record tells of one Captain Otto Van Tyle, a privateer, who was at least accused of being one of Kidd's men, foundering off Sandy Hook in the privateer *Castle Del Key,* December 24, 1705. Of the 145 men clinging to her shrouds in the sub-zero weather, only four lived. Was he one of them? We will likely never know.

But up in Toms River, there is a little island, capped today by a number of stately homes, that bears the interesting name of Money Island. Here, it is rumored, lies part of Kidd's lost treasure, and, during the 19th century, gold-diggers pocked the summit with their exploratory excavations. No one, as far as it is known, came up with anything of value. Yet, who knows? Whatever they sought may still lie a bit below someone's cellar floor. What truth the tale may have can only be judged by the diligence of those seekers in the 1800s. Perhaps the following segment, related to the foraging, can be looked at less skeptically.

F. Alexander Lucas, in his 1911 fictional publication *Barnegat Yarns*, strikes up a friendship with a most-elderly Long Beach local and, in the course of time, exhumes from his faded memory an old family tale which he definitely associates with the Kidd saga. It begins one dark night in the early 18th century, when a local was plying his trade in a skiff somewhere south of Barnegat Inlet on the bay. A longboat was seen to approach him from the north, moving under muffled oars with obvious caution. The observer followed it to a spot one mile south of "the cedars" where the crew landed on the marsh along the bay. Creeping through the dunes, having likewise left his boat, the observer discerned the feeble glow of a lantern and, there "in the shadow of the Old Hawk Tree" he watched them bury a chest and cover it with a layer of gunpowder and brimstone. The idea was that anyone digging with a steel shovel would strike a spark and be blown to bits. Our observer fled back to his boat, making a narrow escape when one of the secretive group discovered him. Later, at a local tavern, the excited bayman revealed his story; among the listeners was an ancestor of Mr. Lucas's crony. All present apparently vowed to respect the chest's integrity, probably in view of the protective measures its owners had taken. Thus, so far as the legend goes, the chest was allowed to sleep unmolested and the crew that buried it were lost to other devices. It could very well have happened.

Now another tale, from another series of sources, and more accurately documented, can be brought to light. Two and one quarter miles south of Beach Haven, in the 1880s lay a government station of the lifesaving service. During the day of September 11, 1886 a sloop hove-to off the station towards sunset and put over a yawl that pulled through the surf. Two men debarked and walked purposefully to the station where they identified themselves as "surveyors." Inquiring as to the location of "the two cedars," well-known landmarks that stood about one hundred yards above the site of then-closed Old Inlet, they accepted lodging at the station and apparently settled down for the night.

At daybreak, the station lookout spotted the pair digging furiously far down the beach. When a party was sent to investigate, they fled to the yawl, "taking something with them." By the time the party arrived, the interlopers were gone and at the abandoned spot where they had been digging there were two holes and beside one lay a rotten chest, a few old Spanish coins, a map yellowed with age, and a heavy gold-hilted cutlass. It sounds almost too "pat" to be real, but the cutlass hung for many years in the lifesaving headquarters at Asbury Park for all comers to see. Was it Kidd's treasure? I like to think that it was!

The sea is in some respects, and has always been, a highway. The coasts, fraught with shoals and danger, have been traditionally treacherous segments of this water highway, along which waited the highwaymen of piracy. Isolated coasts have long bred a history of pirates: Barbary Coast, the rocky coasts of Britain, Cape Cod with its "Mooncussers." Thus Barnegat beaches claim their own Barnegat pirates.

During the colonial proprietorship, authorities had difficulty even reaching the Jersey shore, let alone maintaining control over it. Moreover, England indulged in the practice of deporting her criminals to the colonies, a custom that continued until a formal protest by Benjamin Franklin late in the 18th century. Many of these men of limited scruples sought refuge on the western frontier or along the isolated coasts. Island Beach, according to Van Sant, became one of the most dreaded spots on the Atlantic seaboard.

Ebenezer Tucker, who fitted out privateers during the Revolution, turned, after the war, to helping shipwreck victims recover belongings "plundered by the unprincipled shallopmen and inhabitants of the coast." Even items of clothing did not appear to be sacred. and poor victims, "unable to defend themselves had little recourse."

English common law, of course, contained provisions relating to the status of shipwrecks, and, much of this code was assimilated in laws adopted by the colonial, and later state, legislatures, but enforcement was at first impractical. Apparently the first legal step on the subject was taken by the New Jersey Legislature on May 31, 1799, authorizing the sheriffs of shore counties to take charge of wrecks in their territories. A "wreck commissioner" was appointed in the early years of the 19th century.

There is perhaps a bit of philosophy that might be introduced justifying, if you will, the pirate element. Most significant was probably the legalization of privateering during wartime by issuing "letters of *marque*.[6]" Understandably the boost given by incoming goods was greatly appreciated by a generally weak local economy, and upon cessation of hostilities, it was hard to see the difference between looting a foundering ship in war or in peace. There were, however, stories of wreckers leading horses down the beach with lights tied to their tails to confuse coasting vessels that they might more conveniently run ashore.

Some felt that the wreckers (looters might be more fair) believed they were justified in claiming what the sea lay before them, and, indeed, what they might well risk life and limb to get regardless of its legal ownership. That in itself seemed obscurely submerged in the common law, about which they had never heard. Likely, the frequency of disaster alongshore had also hardened locals to the sight of human misery. Perhaps this explains the despoilment of corpses which, on occasion, was said to occur.

Indeed, the wrecker's philosophy was incorporated even into their moral fabric. Witness the fisherman's child, taught to pray:

> God bless Mam, Pap,
> And all us poor miserable sinners,
> And send a ship ashore
> Before mornin'.

Piracy: Fact or Fancy?

Tales of Barnegat pirates persisted in creeping inland. When the *Minturn* went ashore in February, 1846 insinuations about plunder grew so pointed that the legislature appointed a committee to investigate the charges. Their findings however, revealed only accounts of heroism and honor. The *Minturn*, for example, had a

[6]*License or commission granted by a state to a private citizen to capture and confiscate the merchant ships of another nation.*

cargo value of $84,000 — all but about $300 of which was accounted for. Tales of false lights were all but discounted.

A foreign brig came ashore during the 19th century near Barnegat Inlet. Her survivors, armed to the teeth in defense against pirates, which the crew were sure they would find, approached members of the Woodmansee family who cared for them admirably. "I don't know as I've ever been used to better," stated her captain.

But were the tales all false? I don't think we can shrug off the incidents surrounding the grounding of the *George Cameron* off Absecon, when, even after the looting was done, neighbor stole from neighbor in a wild orgy of greed. One looter would bury what he could not carry behind a dune. While he was running off for more loot, another would come along and dig up what the first had left behind. Two persons were left on the beach to die that wild night. We must admit that what depredations did occur were rare, and served to hurt those devoted Islanders to whom hundreds owed their lives. Frankly, can we say much more for people today?

The Lifesaving Service

William Newell left the storm-swept dunes of Long Beach Island one night in 1839 a troubled man. He had helplessly watched the brig *Terasto* break up on the bar near the island's Mansion of Health, and seen with his own eyes her thirteen seamen die in the surf. In an address before the New Jersey State Legislature, Newell later said:

> ...these unfortunates might have been saved could a rope have been thrown to their assistance over the fatal chasm a few hundred yards to the bar.

The idea of group rescue, of course, was not unique with Mr. Newell. When the packet *Henry Clay* came in off Mantoloking in 1838, the local wreck commissioner, John B. Forman, signaled her crew to get a hawser ashore. He had a tub rigged on running gear in which her 270 passengers were brought through the surf in twos and threes.

But Newell's experience had nevertheless moved him deeply, and, in 1847, as a congressman from Monmouth County, he secured moderate appropriations for the purchase of Francis Lifecars, rocket-lines, and hawsers to be kept in simple frame structures erected for that purpose along the coast. The first of these shelters was built in 1848 at Spermaceti Cove near Sandy Hook, followed by seven more within a year. Captain Sammy Perrine was keeper of the Harvey Cedars station, erected the same year. Both Captain Perrine and the lifeboat crew were volunteers. It was from this station that a lifeboat was dragged in 1854, for a vain attempt to reach the stranded *Powhattan*. Years later, the remodeled station was floated on a scow down the bay to Beach Haven, where "Tilt" (John Tilton) Fox, jacked it up on piles as the Hotel de Crab in 1872. Wholly enveloped by modern additions, it was still standing in 1966.

There was a similar station near Bond's resort, also, in the early days unmanned, and the key to the boathouse was kept hanging in Bond's bar. Whenever a wreck occurred, Captain Bond would muster the more able and courageous of his guests and they would drag out the lifeboat for a dramatic rescue. During the early 1850s a ship named the *Georgia* came ashore carrying about four hundred immigrants. All of them were finally rescued but Bond found

The original Harvey Cedars Life-saving Station, erected in 1848, was enlarged in 1871 when keeper J. Warner Kinsey was in charge

them so famished that he had to stand guard with an ax at the doorway to his kitchen until food could be prepared.

Newell's ideas brought together the Francis Lifecar and a line-throwing mortar or "Parrot Rifle" (a cannon), which weighed 266-pounds and had a range of 470-yards. The first use of the "Newell Apparatus" came on an icy January 12, 1850, when the Scottish brig *Ayreshire*, carrying 201 English and Irish immigrants, was bilged on the bar off Squan Beach and lost her masts.

A seaman named John Maxson, from the local station, jockeyed his mortar into position and fired the first line. His carrying projectile bedded itself neatly in a timber of the *Ayreshire*. Using the light line, her crew hauled out a hawser and tackle upon which the lifecar was run. Again and again it made this perilous journey until two hundred souls stood, shivering but safe, on the beach. The only man lost was a single passenger who, refusing to use the lifecar, died in the icy surf trying to swim ashore.

A few days later, the *Ayreshire* hulk having been scattered by the surf, a beach stroller came upon Maxson's well-placed projectile, still imbedded in the timber, which had washed ashore. It is preserved today in Washington's Smithsonian Institution. Original lifecars are displayed at the Highlands Twin Lights Museum and the Tuckerton Seaport.

Expansion of the Service

A station was erected at Bay Head in 1874. It was a one-story building, framed of local pine, 18 x 36-feet on a foundation of brick. If it conformed with the policy of most early stations, it was painted barn-red and, initially, had only a single room where the surfboat and gear would be stored. For some reason, the Bay Head station faced a windowless end toward the southwest.

Lifesaving stations, at their inception were — as we have said — unmanned and, all too often, the gear was converted to private use while ships went to pieces in view of a station existing only in name. In 1854, a paid keeper was assigned, but not until 1871 were permanent crews recruited, usually from the ranks of the surf-wise pound fishermen of the shore. Stations were modified to fill these new requirements. A kitchen was walled off and sleeping quarters likewise partitioned from the main storage area. Bay Head, in 1883, had three rooms and a loft above. Usually there was a cupola set up for the lookout. A crew was on twenty-four hour call through the wreck season that lasted approximately from September 1 until May 1. The size of a crew was determined generally by the number required to man the station's largest boat, usually six. An extra customarily came on to tend shore duties each December 1st.

These were tough men, and dedicated: "The book said you have to go out, but it didn't say anything about coming back!" commented one lifesaving service man.

When the lookout, or a breathless local, reported a ship ashore, the crew would turn out, no matter what the hour, and usually in the most bitter weather imaginable . They dragged out their boat, always kept ready on a high, wide-tired cart, and hauled it, often for exhausting miles through soft sand. There were no roads whatever on the barrier islands in those days.

It is hard to describe the barrier beach at night during a gale to someone who has not experienced its biting winter fury. The wind planes off the beach and sweeps before it a cutting barrage of skin-slicing grains so fierce you cannot face into it without physical pain. You stumble rather than walk, buffeted by the wind, and the very earth trembles under the shock of booming surf. With the excruciating cold and salt rime-ice forming where the waves deposit their foam, I have watched it in darkened awe as great masses of grey-brown water heaved up to 12- and 14-feet before crashing with the staccato *CRUMP!* and a rumble like distant artillery. I cannot conceive how men could face this in small boats.

But they did, when for one reason or another, the line and gun would not suffice, often waiting hours for a break in the surf, poised there on the brink with numbing icewater swirling about (and likely into) their boots.

"Shove her in!" shouted the keeper.

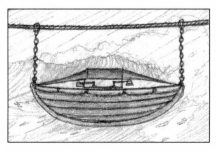

Number 1 and 2 surfmen bounded to the bow and took their oars, holding her head to the sea. The rest pressed her on until she cleared the bottom, then swung aboard and pulled like all hell. The station keeper stood at the big aft oar, tense-

Sketch of the Francis Lifecar.

faced, studying the making surf before them. More than once they miscalculated and rolled their boat under. More than once men died, but the book said what it said and nothing more.

By 1872 stations of the lifesaving service were spaced at an average of five miles. The unwieldy parrot rifles were eventually replaced by the Lyle gun, which weighed only 185 pounds and had a range of 965 yards. It had been designed by Colonel A.D. Lyle (U.S. Army) and fired a projectile 14 1/2-inches long. In loading, the projectile was inserted nose-down into the cannon's muzzle and, when fired, inverted in flight as it peeled line from a special rack.

The breeches buoy, perhaps best described as a refinement on Mr. Forman's "tub," surprisingly, did not come into use until some years after the lifecar. It was characterized by a large cork ring-buoy from which hung a generous pair of canvas "breeches" to take the passenger's legs. It was supposedly first employed on the *Antioch* wreck off Manasquan.

What progress had the service achieved? Between 1871 and 1877, 322 ships were wrecked on the Jersey Shore, with a total of 6,327 people aboard. Only fifty-five were lost, a score of 99.2 percent, and in 1890, of those aboard 62 wrecks, there were no deaths.

The year 1900 saw forty-two stations along the shore at an average spacing of three miles. Many of the early frame buildings had been supplanted by larger more comprehensive structures. A second erection at Bay Head had even been torn down and replaced by a third, which stands today on Route 35, a block behind a renowned local pub, the Bluffs.[7]

[7] The old station stands in year 2000 but the Bluffs is, sadly, gone.

Since the late 18th century, our government had maintained a protective arm, known as the Revenue Cutter Service, to protect the coasts from smugglers and piracy. On January 28, 1915, this was merged with the U. S. Life Saving Service to form the United States Coast Guard, which stands today as one of our major arms of national defense. Within the framework of the Coast Guard, however, the lifesaving service maintained its stations, equipment, and, indeed, the heritage it had earned through sixty-eight heroic years.

One generally considers the days of shipwreck to be over, but the Coast Guard's duties have merely been compounded. There is still, as we have discussed, a large commercial fleet to be shepherded, and the boating boom of the fifties had created new problems from amateur boatmen, including water safety violations, and pollution incidents.

The Saga of Old Barney

Since long before the days of Karlsefni, Gomez, and Juet, Barnegat Inlet has spewed out her angry tides across the shoals twice daily. Small wonder that when men had to contend with them, having only inadequate charts and the tenuous approximation of position that is so often the lot of "bluewater" sailors, they should seek to warn their fellows of such hazard. This, accordingly, is the story of Barnegat Light, "Grand Old Champion of the Tides."

The story, as is usually the case in such chronicles, begins not with "Old Barney" but in 1834, when Congress squeezed out $6,000 for the erection of a 50-foot lighthouse of whitewashed brick on the inlet's shore. A publication of the Long Beach Board of Trade indicates that while the structure was whitewashed from top to bottom, all the exposed metal surfaces had been finished flat black. The light itself was "fixed;" that is, unblinking, and whale oil was used for illumination. In 1855, a new, more powerful beacon was installed, but, only a year later, the tides undercut the foundation of the tower and it toppled into the inlet. The keeper, James Fuller, and his family had been living in a dwelling only 60-feet west of the light, and, upon this nerve shattering event, they moved into the base of a wooden tower that was hastily erected nearby and lit with lamps salvaged from the old light.

Still determined, Congress sent Lieutenant George Meade (later the General Meade of Civil War fame) and $60,000 to the shores of turbulent Barnegat Inlet. Shortly, removed about half a mile from the original site and at exactly latitude 39° 6' 54", and longitude 74° 6' 1", a new lighthouse rose on foundations utilizing the most modern principles for stability. Its walls were ten feet thick at the base and tapered to eighteen inches at the top, a lofty 168-feet above sea level. The tower was completed in 1858 at a cost of $45,000 — standing second in the United States only to Pensacola Light in Florida, which is twelve inches higher.

A heavy iron pipe ran from the ground to the base of the light mechanism. Around this spiraled 217 cast-iron steps. Windows opened along the staircase at all points of the compass. At each side of the lower door were spaces for equipment storage, and, above, a shelf-lined office for the keeper.

At the tower's summit was a circular platform and glass enclosure containing the $15,000 light mechanism, keynoted by a kerosene burner with five concentric circular wicks of one, two, three, four and five inch diameter. From a 10-gallon reservoir they consumed 4.5 gallons a night in summer, 7.5 gallons in winter. Some 2,500 gallons a year found its way through the illuminating devices. The vast lens was 7-inches thick, 8-feet in diameter and 15-feet high. The device incorporated 1,024 cylindrical prisms after the design of Augustin Fresnel, which had been formed in the French furnaces of St. Gobian. They were assembled by Henri Lepaute of Paris. The whole apparatus, weighing some five tons, rested on bronze rollers so finely balanced that it could be turned with a finger. In practice it was rotated once each four minutes by a clock-like mechanism running by the impetus of a 150 pound weight which was suspended by a 65-foot cable running in the hollow center pipe. It had to be wound up each hour.

Barnegat Light emitted a 16,000-candlepower flash of the "first order" every ten seconds. With the light plane at 163 feet, its visibility, in clear weather, was limited only by the curvature of the earth. From the deck aboard ship it could be seen 25 miles; from the masthead, thirty. The generally attributed visibility, owing to atmospheric haze, was 19 or 20 miles, with the observer at sea level.

A tale is told of one Tilden Estlow who was jacking deer with some friends one night on the "plains" above the Mullica. Their lights picked up a single reflected eye in the brush and, maneuvering cautiously to get a clear shot, they fired repeated salvos before discovering their attempts were directed at Barnegat Light, many miles away! Under more immediate influence of the light, migratory brant geese often became confused in their flight and, striking the glass, fell dead to the ground, often in such numbers as to cover the sand with their bodies.

During heavy Atlantic gales, the tower actually shuddered and swayed so violently that a bucket of water placed on the platform would nearly empty itself. In such storms, the light mechanism sometimes failed to operate and the keeper on watch had to go up and turn it by hand. I have stood atop the light on the heels of a gale when gusts were hitting at perhaps fifty miles per hour. The roar of wind was deafening and the vibration made one's very thoughts quiver. The man on watch could never leave his post until replaced, and felt relief only when a slow tread advanced up the spiral, breaking into his narrow sphere of roaring wind, slow swirl-flash of light, and rumbling gearwork. The watches ran from sundown to 10 P.M., 10 P.M. to 2 P.M., and 2 P.M. to sunrise.

Barnegat Light stood thus, a most compelling symbol on the Jersey Shore. Her beam was unflagging except once during the Civil War when the lens was removed and buried in the dunes to prevent its capture by Confederate raiders who had, at least on one occasion, penetrated to New Jersey soil. In 1889, $12,000 was spent erecting a spacious house for the keeper. A 1914 photograph show both the light and keeper's residence, a good distance from the swirling tide and sandbar on the inlet's south shore. Rapid southerly migration of the channel, however, continued to encroach and, before many years, the keeper's house toppled into the sea. It was perhaps due to this advancing jeopardy that subsequent to World War I rumors circulated that the tower would be replaced by a lightship in the sea lanes.

In 1920, locals, who revered the lighthouse both as a landmark and steering point for their fishing vessels, literally raised their own taxes to move in auto-wrecks that were pushed into the inlet as a breakwater to save the federal structure from collapse. In 1926, virtually abandoned by the government, Old Barney was sold to the state for $1.

As the fates decreed, *Barnegat* Lightship was placed in operation on August 15, 1927, eight miles offshore. She was moored in twelve fathoms of water, with two giant "mushroom" anchors of 7,000 and 7,500 pounds, riding to 120 fathoms of 1 5/8-inch chain. *Barnegat* is 113-feet long, with black topsides, and displaces 565 tons.

Her 15,000 candlepower light rides a masthead 65-feet above the water, emitting a white flash every ten seconds with a two-second "eclipse," and is visible for twelve miles. Other instrumentation include a radio navigation beacon, 12-inch steam chime (a form of foghorn), and an underwater bell. Although the lightship is well offshore, its visible range is approximately the same as the old lighthouse. Since the ship requires nine men and five officers to staff (where the lighthouse took never more than three), it is probably these additional navigational aids that justify her existence.

With the installation of the lightship, the illuminating complex was removed from Barnegat Lighthouse and was eventually displayed in the Rosenwald Museum of Science in Chicago. It was replaced by an 800-pound acetylene gas blinker, mounted atop the cupola roof like "a wart on a pickle" (to quote a contemporary view). It was designed to burn six months without refueling but, typically, a few weeks after its installation electricity reached Barnegat City. It was replaced by a naked 250-watt bulb, which though its lightplane was 13-feet higher than the original light, emits a "feeble" eight-mile beam.

Tides eventually erased the auto-wreck breakwater, and only a few years prior to the lighthouse's centennial was reasonably adequate bulkheading erected. In 1958, its hundredth year, the light was opened to the public and, for the inevitable fee, you may burst your blood vessels climbing the 217 steps to the summit, now caged protectively in wire grid with ever-watchful attendants clustering about. In fair weather there is an admirable view of Long Beach Island, the inlet, and, seaward, the timeless shoals, which break only in heavy weather.[8]

[8] *Today, there is no fee to climb to the top of the lighthouse, and it is open every day.*

The lens has been removed from its repose in Chicago and is again on display in Barnegat Light[9], but no longer does it blink out a warning to the seafarer. For the old sentinel, there remains only a lightless eye to stare out on its memories as the second century creeps by.

[9] *Today the lens is in the Barnegat Light Museum, run by the Historical Society in an old one-room schoolhouse.*

A Fated Rival

There was another light serving the Barnegat area built on Tucker's Island in 1848, at the mouth of Little Egg Harbor and the Mullica. Its operation, for reasons undefined, appears to have been discontinued between 1859 and 1867. Following that it burned steadily, "known to all seamen" frequenting the shores. Prior to World War I, Tucker's Beach had fifteen residents and a lifesaving station with eight crewmen. The light was kept by Arthur Rider. In 1927, beach erosion, apparent nemesis of all but the most secure lighthouses, toppled Mr. Rider's employment into the sea. Little Egg Harbor Lighthouse was replaced briefly with a blinker on a steel tower. In a storm one night the lifesaving station was washed away and, in time, the residents, threatened by further erosion, left their homes to stand bare-shingled and empty-eyed until they too succumbed. In a few decades the little island itself followed them.

Some History Revived

The time: an indefinite date before 1810. The place: Squan Beach, just above Manasquan Inlet. It is night but the sands are alight with a ruddy glow. A ship is burning off the coast. She is a 100-foot British merchantman bearing general cargo, probably bound for New York. Her hold is filled with iron-hooped wooden casks of hardware: brass doorknobs, buttons marked "London-Extra Rich," hinges, padlocks, scissors, silver spoons, augers for boring, muskrat traps, and a wide assortment of early Sheffield cutlery including many matched bone-handled sets by William Greaves and Sons.

[10]Researcher John Bandstra of the New Jersey Historical Divers Association has since identified this wreck as the Black Ball packet ship Amity, inbound from Liverpool under Captain W. Pease, and lost in 1824.

Lying well over, she is consumed to the waterline and her blazing remains slide under to be quenched forever in a roil of bubbling vapor 250 yards from the beach. It is not known what ship she was or who, if anyone, survived. There appeared in my notes the name *Hannah* from a lost source, but I include it here merely as a nuisance, since competent and erudite authority maintains the ship is anonymous.[10]

There was the Italian merchant vessel *Civita Carrara* wrecked at nearly the same spot, 150 yards further offshore, possibly between 1820 and 1830,[11] while bound for an American port from the Mediterranean. Her cargo included hand-forged iron harness chains from Italy, nested pots hand spun from brass discs in Morocco, and a shipment of 70-pound tin ingots, assayed at 99.8 percent pure. We know nothing of the circumstances under which this ship met her end. Thus two ships lay unmarked, decomposing in their common aquatic crypt for a century and a half.

[11]Bandstra reports this as 1888.

During World War II, a heavy storm disturbed the *Carrara* wreck, scattering her cargo across the sea floor to mingle, in part, with that of the British vessel. Unburdened, a section of this ruptured hull apparently moved inshore, and, with a subsequent storm, was cast upon the beach. Copper was in demand during those years of privation. Planks of the old ship, sheathed with copper to protect against shipworms, were soon stripped to the naked wood. Not to be thus shamed *Carrara*'s remains, under the impetus of drifting sand and tidal suction, settled down and out of sight, where it is said, they may be found today.

Again, all was forgotten until, on July 3, 1955, some fishermen fouled their lines on an underwater object. One of the group donned skin-diving gear and went down to free it, only to find it tangled in an ancient and twisted mass of cargo rising 12-feet from a bottom of blue clay 30 feet down. The British ship had come to light. The excited group returned through the summer and brought up artifacts and photographs of their discovery. Their exploration likewise revealed the *Carrara* site further offshore. Little then remained of either vessel and the cargoes was cemented together in a solid mass of corrosion.

The issue thus reposed until the fall of 1956, when another group brought a commercial fisher dragger on the scene and began operations. The initial discoverers protested. Suddenly, two forgotten ships, 150-years old, became bones of legal contention.

Hardly had the case opened when the issue of government rights was introduced. The federal government had no claim, since neither was a government ship, nor carried (so far as could be determined) government cargoes. Nevertheless, someone dug deep in Trenton and came up with a remnant of the common law stating that any wreck inshore, which lay unclaimed for a year and a day, became the property of the Crown. Contemporary interpretation, strangely, relegated the proceeds of such windfalls to the public school system, and, since it was difficult to imagine that nebulous organization mustering its resources for undersea salvage, a thorny issue remained. At any rate, the original group of divers were appointed to complete the salvage of the vessels for our magnanimous state.

On January 18, 1958, some 250 items, representing only a fourth of the cargo, were auctioned by the Bureau of Navigation in Point Pleasant for the sum of $1,671. Some five hundred persons came by, most to gape, and someone bought the 8,500 "Extra Rich" buttons at $4 per hundred. A while back you could get them as souvenirs at the Barnegat Light Museum.

The legal pot continued to boil for the next five years, and slowly a muddled policy evolved of issuing "salvage permits" on coastal wrecks, with a percentage of the take reverting to the state. Concern, however, mounted over the poor archaeological discipline of amateur salvagers, and the infinite damage they might do to valuable wrecks which might otherwise contribute immeasurably to our knowledge of the past. And still the question of legitimate title was unresolved: indeed its complex horizons had widened.

In the spring of 1963, a symposium was held on this subject under the sponsorship of the American Littoral Society. Tentative steps at least were taken with the establishment of a "wreck index" at the Sandy Hook Marine Laboratory and the founding of the *San Diego* Fund (named after a U.S. warship torpedoed off New England) to preserve undersea wrecks for their historical significance and as marine life habitats. Divers, fishing interests and historical sources contribute data on various sites as they come to light, with the hope of establishing a comprehensive inventory.

With the era of frequent shipwrecks mercifully at end, there is potential that these ships may not always lie fallow on the rolls of anonymity. With industrious application, they may well bequeath us insights into the life and employment of other times, and may themselves gain the dignity, or ignominy, of light thrown upon the dark termination of so many hopeful voyages.

Acknowledgments

I cannot say the present work grew solely from my own inspiration. Appraised of my interest in historical material, my late uncle Robert Morris DuFour pointed me to John Cunningham's revealing series in the Newark Sunday News and started two years in the catacombs of Rutgers University's magnificent library, which labor turned up what now comprises a major portion of this book. Failing somewhat by 1958 under the rigors of producing an anywhere-near scholarly work, I soon owed much of my inspiration to Martha Clayton Neary, who took me to the Ocean County Library and shared the benefit of her family's two generations at the shore. My long suffering mother kindly proofed much of the original text.

2002

Closed Sea owes its resurrection and life as a published work to many people other than its author. Terry O'Leary, then managing Tuckerton Seaport's Barnegat Bay Decoy & Baymen's Museum, first proposed printing this book after I donated a photocopy of the original manuscript to their library. His creativity and enthusiasm got the project moving. Carolyn Campbell and her wonderful colleagues at the Ocean County Historical Society, read the manuscript, endorsed its publication and greatly helped me edit and update critical facts. The obstacles to publishing were made possible by a most welcome grant from the Barnegat Bay Estuary Program. Current Tuckerton Seaport Program Coordinator Patricia A. Schuster, and dedicated former staff members Mary Jerkowicz, Dottie VonTronk, and volunteer Joan Kingman, all gave of their own time and diligence to make this aging, pre-computer, hard copy manuscript accessible for modern publishing. Finally, Perdita Buchan, shore resident and Pine Barrens afficionado, edited the purple prose of my youth with an understanding hand. All these colleagues were a complete delight with whom to work and I send *Closed Sea* to the printer calling all of them friends! My mother, Dorothy Mountford Sage — she married our respected family dentist after Dad's death in 1981 — still lives and prospers on the Jersey Shore. She celebrates her 90th birthday as this manuscript goes to press.

Bibliography

Feeling some moral compulsion to give credit to laboring artists of the past, I have compiled below a selected bibliography from which virtually all my information has been drawn:

Maps

Cook, George H. (State Geologist); and Vermeule, C.C. (topographer). *Topographical Map of the Vicinity of Barnegat Bay.* 1889.

de Velasco, Don Alonso. *The de Velasco Chart.* Spain, 1611.

Green, Mildred C. *A Romance Map of New Jersey.* Buffalo, N.Y. Whitney Graham Inc., 1935.

Jefferies, Thomas, Geographer to H.R.H. Prince of Wales. *The Middle British Colonies in America.* London: 1771 (copy from a map made in Philadelphia, 1755).

Lea, Phillip. *The Phillip Lea Chart.* Cheapside, London: 1690.

Montanus, Arnoldus. *A Map of New Belgium.* 1671.

The Province of New Jersey — Divided into East and West Commonly called Jerseys. December 1, 1777 (map compiled).

Seller, John; and Fisher, William. *A Map of New Iarsey in America.* London: 1676 or 1677

United States Coast and Geodetic Survey. Charts No. (825) Sandy Hook to Little Egg Harbor, 1956, and (1216) Sea Girt to Little Egg Inlet, 1953.

Vanderdonck, Adrian. Untitled map of Jersey area. 1600s.

Worlidge, John. *A Map of East and West Jersey, as surveyed by* ...(etc.). London: around 1700.

Periodicals

The Asbury Park Evening Press. Asbury Park, New Jersey.

The National Geographic Magazine. Organ of the National Geographic Society. Washington, D.C. Special reference to: Long, John E.. *New Jersey Now.* May, 1933; Klingle, G.C. and Culver, W.R. *One Hundred Hours Beneath the Chesapeake.* May, 1955; Smith, F.G.Walton, and Sisson, R.F. *Shipworms, Saboteurs of the Sea.* October, 1956.

The Newark Evening News. Newark, New Jersey.

The Newark Sunday News. Newark, New Jersey. Cunningham, John T. *The Barnegat Peninsula.* March 24, 1957; *Island at Sea.* March 31, 1957; *The Hungry Sea.* April 2, 1957; *Fishing for Fun.* June 16, 1957; *Treasure Trove.* June 23, 1957; Kennet, Warren H. *Atlantic's Graveyard.* August 1, 1954.

The Plainfield Courier News. Plainfield, New Jersey.

Report From Rutgers. Vol. XI, No. 9. New Brunswick, New Jersey: November, 1959. (Contains a fine article on malaria and the encephalitis infestation of 1959).

Sea Frontiers. Bulletin of the International Oceanographic Foundation, with reference to two specific articles: Smith, F.G. Walton. *Flying Barnacles.* September, 1957; Dickson, Fred J. *Estuary and Marsh.* February, 1958.

Books and Other Publications
American Wildlife. New York: William H. Wise & Co., 1954.
Barclay, John; and Forbes, Arthur. (Testimony thereof) March 29, 1684.
Beck, Henry Charlton. *Fare to Midlands.* New York: Dutton and Co., 1939.
————————— . *Jersey Genesis.* New Brunswick, New Jersey: Rutgers University Press, 1945.
————————— . *More Forgotten Towns of Southern New Jersey.* New York: E.P. Dutton, 1937.
————————— . *The Roads of Home.* New Brunswick, New Jersey: Rutgers University Press, 1957.
Blunt, Edmund M. *Blunt's American Coast Pilot.* New York: editions of 1815 and 1827.
Brick Township Chamber of Commerce. *1957 Official Guide to Brick Township.*
Burton, Maurice. *Margins of the Sea.* New York: 1954.
Carson, Rachel L. *Fish and Shellfish of the Middle Atlantic Coast.* Conservation Bulletin No. 38. Washington, D.C.: U.S. Government Printing Office, 1945.
Chase Manhattan Bank. *Moneys of the World.* Reprint, 1958.
Crowder, William. Between *the Tides.* New York: 1931.
Cunningham, John T. *Garden State.* Rutgers University Press, 1955
————————— . *The New Jersey Shore,* New Brunswick, New Jersey: Rutgers University Press, 1958.
Davies, Stanley Powell. *Social Control of the Mentally Deficient.* Thomas Y. Crowell, 1930.
DeVaet, J. *Nieuwe Werelt.* Edition of 1625.
Federal Writer's Project of the W.P.A. *Stories of New Jersey.* New York: M. Barrows and Co., 1938. Also published in Newark, New Jersey, 1938-39, 1939-42 and 1942.
Flink, Solomon J. *The Economy of New Jersey.* New Brunswick, New Jersey: Rutgers University Press, 1958.
Heilprin, Angelo. *The Animal Life of Our Seashore.* Philadelphia: 1888.
Heston, Alfred Miller. *South Jersey, a History.* Vols. I and II, New York: Lewis Historical Publishing Company, 1924.
Juet, Robert. *Mr. Hendrick Hudson's Derde Reize Onder Nederlandsche Vlag, Van Amsterdam Naar Nova Zembla, America, En Terug Naar Dartmouth, England.* Robert Juet, Lime House, 1609.
Kite, Elizabeth. *Report on Social Conditions in the Pine Belt.* Trenton, New Jersey: 1913. (Interesting, but possibly overdone)
Kobbe, Gustav. *The Jersey Coast and Pines.* Short Hills, New Jersey: 1889.
Larison, Cornelius Wilson. The *Tenting School, a Description of Tours Taken, (etc.)...* Ringoes, New Jersey: C.W. Larison, 1883.
Long Beach Island Business Directory and Guide Book. New Jersey: Long Beach Board of Trade, 1959.
Lucas, F. Alexander. *Barnegat Yarns.* New York: Broadway Publishing Co., 1911.
Murphy, Henry C. *The Voyage of Verrazzano.* New York: 1875.
Naber, S.P. L'Honore'. Preface to reprint of Juet's writings, Martinus Nijhaff, 1921.
Nash, Charles Edgar. *The Lure of Long Beach.* New Jersey: Long Beach Board of Trade, 1936.
Nelson, William. (editor) The *Jersey Coast in Three Centuries.* New York, Chicago: Lewis Historical Publishing Company, 1902.
Ocean County Chosen Board of Freeholders. *Barnegat Light, Grand Old Champion of the Tides.* issued through the Bureau of Publicity, Toms River, New Jersey: 1957-58.
Pearson, Hayedn S. Sea *Flavor.* New York: Whittlesey House, 1948.

Pierce, Arthur Dudley. *Iron in the Pines*. New Brunswick, New Jersey: Rutgers University Press, 1957.

Pohl, Frederick Julius. The *Lost Discovery*. New York: W.W. Norton Co., Inc., 1952.

Richardson, A.P. *Barnegat Ways*. New York and London: Century Company, 1931. (Mr. Richardson used to own a boatyard at Mantoloking and consequently has a fond insight into the bay).

Rose, T.F. *A Historical and Biographical Atlas of the New Jersey Coast*. Philadelphia: Woolman and Rose, 1878.

Schoettle, Edwin D. *Sailing Craft*. Macmillan Company, 1928; Crabbe, Edward. *The Toms River Cup*. Dale, Orton G. *Barnegat Bay Sneakboxes*. Lucke, C.E. Jr. *Fifteen Foot Sneakboxes and Junior Sailing on Barnegat Bay*. Schoettle, Edwin D. *Ice Boating* .

Smith, Samuel. *History of the Colony Of Nova Carsaria*. 1765, with reference to map No. 1, drawn in 1747.

Somerville, George B. *The Lure of Long Beach*. New Jersey: Long Beach Board of Trade, 1914.

Tides of Time in Ocean County. Ocean County (New Jersey) Principal's Council, 1940.

Townsend, Charles Wendell. *Sand Dunes and Salt Marshes*. Boston. L.C. Page and Company, 1925.

Townsend, F.P. *Tel-News*. Monthly publication of the New Jersey Bell Telephone Company.

VanSant, Howard D. *Barnegat Pirates*. (a novel, but of interest). New York: F. Tennyson Neelt, 1897.

Walnut, Aylward J. *A Study of Long Beach Island, New Jersey*. (unpublished Master thesis) Submitted to Columbian College of George Washington University, October, 1956.

Washington, General George. Original *Letter to General Forman*. October 19, 1777.

Weygandt, Cornelius. *Down Jersey*. New York, London: D. Appelton Century Co., 1940.

Wilson, Harold Fisher. *The Jersey Shore*. Vols. I and II. New York: Lewis Historical Publishing Company, 1953.

(Note: The following series are of great interest to the nature lover who will frequent the shore. I have found them of more use than I care to admit! The ubiquitous Dr. Zim appears to have a finger in every pie here.)

Zim, Herbert, and Ingle, Lester. *Seashores*. New York: Simon and Schuster, 1955.

Zim, Herbert, and Gabrielson, Ira N. *Birds*, New York: Simon and Schuster, 1949.

Zim, Herbert, and Martin, Alexander C. *Flowers*. New York: Simon and Schuster, 1950.

Zim, Herbert, and Shoemaker, Hurst S. *Fishes*. New York: Simon and Schuster, 1956.

Almost to a letter, these works are available through the Library of Rutgers University, New Brunswick, New Jersey or through the Ocean County Library, Toms River, New Jersey. The New Jersey room of Rutgers' Library contains a wealth of information on the state's history, including countless old maps and volumes.

Index

About the Author

An estuarine ecologist and environmental historian, Kent Mountford, PhD.,
spent 36 years studying North America's Atlantic estuaries. While studying the
then-polluted Potomac River for the District of Columbia government in 1980,
he pioneered the concept of investigating a region's early colonial literature in
order to better understand its current problems. A popular speaker and writer,
Dr. Mountford currently lives and works on the Chesapeake Bay, returning to
Manasquan often, where the family home still stands near Barnegat Bay.

Down The Shore Publishing specializes in books, calendars, cards and videos
about New Jersey and the Shore. For a free catalog of all our titles or to be
included on our mailing list, just send us a request.

Down The Shore Publishing
Box 100, West Creek, NJ 08092

downshore@gmail.com

www.down-the-shore.com

Made in United States
North Haven, CT
03 June 2024

53266804R10126